6.95

N

CONNECTIONS WITH
**THAMES VALLEY**
TRACTION COMPANY LTD.

FROXFIELD
FOREST HOSR
HUNGERFORD
17 14
16
GREAT BEDWYN
15
SHALBOURNE
WILTON
MARTEN 14 15
COMBE 17 17 OXENWOOD
TIDCOMBE LINKENHOLT
FOSBURY
VERNHAM DEAN
82
KINGSTON CONHOLT
COLLINGBOURNE DUCIS
82 UPTON
TANGLEY
Chute
LUDGERSHALL
73
REDENHAM
CLANVILLE
KIMPTON 75 73
WEYHILL
MONXTON
BELLINGER 71
AMPORT
ABBOTTS ANN
ST JOHN'S CROSS
79
Grateley 77 80
LOWER CLATFORD
83
WHERWELL
16
OVER WALLOP 77
MIDDLE WALLOP
LONGSTOCK
83 LECKFORD
NETHER WALLOP
STOCKBRIDGE
CHILBOLTON
BARTON STACEY
ANDOVER
83
CHARLTON
77 72
PICKET PIECE
ENHAM
80
82
HURSTBOURNE TARRANT
135
NETHERTON
80
80
135
FACCOMBE
ASHMANSWORTH
HIGHCLERE
HIGHCLERE COMMON STATION
BURGHCLERE
WHITWAY
80
NEWTOWN
WASH COMMON
122
135
NEWBURY
Thatcham Midgham
BEENHAM
ALDERMASTON STATION
ALDERMASTON VILLAGE
136
BAUGHURST ESTATE
137 115 134
SILCHESTER
TADLEY
BAUGHURST VILLAGE
134 136
BEARSBRIDGE
136
RAMSDEL 137
BRAMLEY
BRAMLEY CAMP
101
134
KINGSCLERE
122
WOLVERTON
MONK SHERBORNE
76 102 103
HANNINGTON
LITCHFIELD
121
NORTH OAKLEY
PARK PREWETT
WOOTTON ST. LAWRENCE
122
136
SHERBORNE ST JOHN
LYDE GREEN
ROTHERWICK TURNING
117
BASING
NEWNHAM
To London
135
Overton
OVERTON MILLS
OVERTON
LAVERSTOKE
WORTING
BASINGSTOKE
STAGE HOUNDS
HACKWOOD PARK
117
76 102
102 76
WHITCHURCH
76 102
HURSTBOURNE PRIORS
LONG PARISH
N. WALTHAM
POPHAM
Michaeldever
103
EAST OAKLEY
111
CLIDDESDEN
WINSLADE
ELLISFIELD
107
HERRIARD
SOUTHROPE
LASHAM
109
DUMMER
109
AXFORD
BARTON STACEY CAMP
BULLINGTON CROSS
BARTON STACEY
SUTTON SCOTNEY
STRATTON PARK
109
PRESTON CANDOVER
BENTWORTH
HOLT END
107
BEECH
ALTON STATION
ALTON
BEECH ABBEY
107
MEDSTEAD
107
WIELD
109
BROWN CANDOVER
SWARRATON
LUNWAYS INN
111
To London

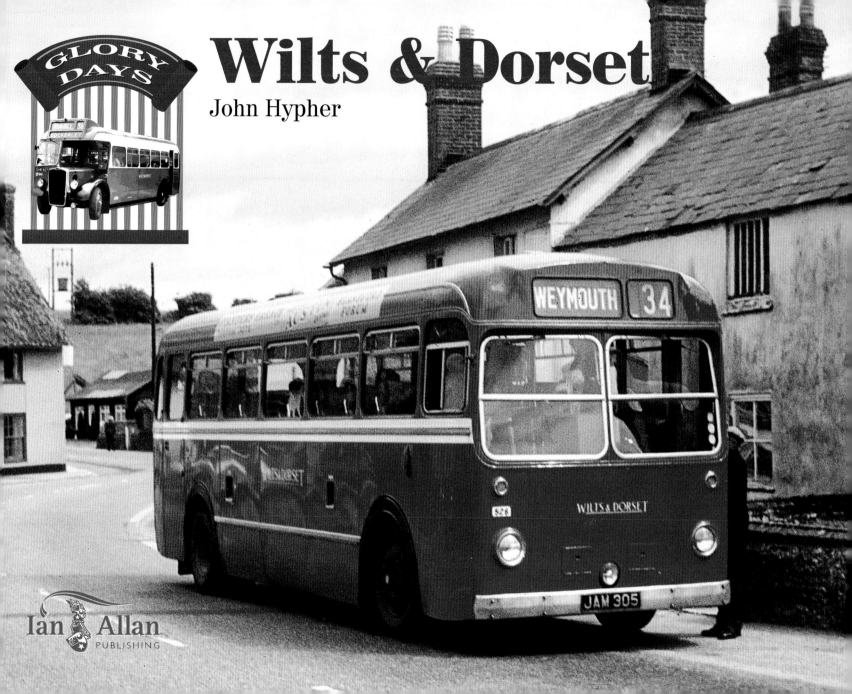

# GLORY DAYS

# Wilts & Dorset

John Hypher

WEYMOUTH 34

WILTS & DORSET

JAM 305

Ian Allan PUBLISHING

*Front cover:*
**Pulling into Wilts &
Dorset's yard in Castle
Street, Salisbury in October
1967 is Bristol LS6G 535
(JMR 13) of February 1953,
which was delivered in the
fine maroon, red and cream
coach livery. It lost its rear
exit in December 1954 and
was later converted to one-
man operation before being
renumbered 758 in 1971.**
*David Mant*

*Back cover:*
**Seen in Marlborough High
Street is Bristol MW6G
836 (EMR 301D) with
ECW 41-seat dual-purpose
bodywork. New in June
1966 and renumbered from
727 in September 1971, this
vehicle became part of the
Hants & Dorset fleet in
October 1972.** *Photobus*

*Title page:*
**Bristol LS6G 526 (JAM
305), new in November
1952, is pictured at
Milborne St Andrew while
working the Weymouth
service in July 1968. Built
with both front and rear
entrance/ exits, it lost its
rear doors in April 1955. It
was converted for OMO in
August 1958, renumbered
749 in 1971 and withdrawn
in February 1972.**
*Chris Aston*

# CONTENTS

| | |
|---|---|
| Introduction | 3 |
| 1. From Horses to Horsepower | 4 |
| 2. A private Venture | 6 |
| 3. Under New Ownership | 14 |
| 4. Nationalisation | 31 |
| 5. Postscript | 92 |
| Appendices | |
| 1. Services Operating October 1935 | 93 |
| 2. Services Operating September 1945 | 94 |
| 3. Services Operating May 1962 | 95 |

First published 2007

ISBN (10) 0 7110 3159 2
ISBN (13) 978 0 7110 3159 3

© John Hypher 2007

Published by Ian Allan Publishing

an imprint of Ian Allan Publishing Ltd, Riverdene Business
Park, Hersham, Surrey KT12 4RG
Printed by Ian Allan Printing Ltd, Riverdene Business Park,
Hersham, Surrey KT12 4RG.

Code: 0703/B

Visit the Ian Allan Publishing Ltd website at
www.ianallanpublishing.com

# ACKNOWLEDGEMENTS

My grateful thanks go to the following for their valuable
help in the preparation of this book: David Mant, David
Gillard, Phil Davies, Chris Aston, Maurice Doggett, Mark
Hughes, The Omnibus Society, Simon Butler, the late
Arnold Richardson of Photobus, Alan B. Cross, Colin Caddy,
J. H. Aston, R. H. G. Simpson, Malcolm Keeley of The
Transport Museum, Wythall and the Bristol Vintage Bus
Group for their superb photographs and transparencies and
for their ready willingness in making these available to me.

Also to Norman Aish and Brian Jackson for opening
important doors early in this project and to the National
Archive, and the Omnibus Society Library for access to
their historical records, to Vivien Ross for her help with
these researches and to David Elliott for his detailed
contributions.

My thanks are also extended to the PSV Circle for
kindly allowing me to draw information from their Wilts &
Dorset Fleet History and to its author, David Pennels, for
supplying additional information and allowing me access
to other works of his.

Special thanks go to Maurice Doggett for kindly reading
through the manuscript and for his comments and
corrections, most of which have been incorporated into
this book, and to my wife Lynda for doing all the
complicated work on the computer.

# INTRODUCTION

Christopher Mcateer

More than 30 years have passed since the 'old' Wilts & Dorset faded into oblivion. It was fully integrated with Hants & Dorset during the early 1970s after a history spanning almost six decades. During that time it grew from being a local Salisbury operator, often fighting for survival against local competition, into a concern with routes not only in Wiltshire, but extending into Hampshire, Dorset and Berkshire.

During World War 2, the Wilts & Dorset fleet was greatly enlarged when it acquired around 100 extra buses, mostly double-deckers, to transport construction workers and service personnel to and from massive military developments on Salisbury Plain. Providing transport for the military continued to play a significant part in Wilts & Dorset's operations and a larger-than-average fleet of coaches was maintained for this purpose.

Major expansion into east Hampshire took place in 1950 when the Venture Transport Company of Basingstoke was purchased by the British Transport Commission and fully absorbed by Wilts & Dorset.

Another major independent concern was acquired by the company during 1963 in the shape of the famous Silver Star company of Porton, together with its portfolio of military services to and from Salisbury Plain and its stage service into Salisbury.

Very much a Tilling company, and under Tilling control from 1942, Wilts & Dorset was often overshadowed by its larger group neighbour, Hants & Dorset. The two companies were placed under common management in 1964 and five years later they passed to the National Bus Company. Wilts & Dorset was fully integrated into its sister company during 1972.

This book relates the interesting story of Wilts & Dorset up to its demise as a separate entity in both words and pictures and will take you on a nostalgic journey which I hope you will enjoy.

3

# 1. FROM HORSES TO HORSEPOWER

Moving around from place to place has changed out of all recognition over the last few hundred years. The pace and style of change has varied considerably depending upon entrepreneurial flair, geographic location and economic activity and in many ways Wiltshire, the heartland of Wilts & Dorset (W&D) has been no exception.

For many, local travel fulfilled the needs of much of the populace with nearby markets and market towns providing a focal point for the villages and hamlets in the surrounding area. Visits to the market, either as buyers or sellers, were often made by village-based carriers' waggons where both passengers and goods (and sometimes livestock) travelled together in these rudimentary vehicles. In many cases, all concerned were exposed to the elements and before roads took on any semblance of smoothness, also had to endure a slow and rough ride into the bargain. Many of these roads were little more than country lanes or tracks and the benefits of a somewhat smoother ride were only felt on the approaches to towns where the roads were maintained to a far better standard by the turnpikes.

Salisbury market was considered to be the market in south Wiltshire. Waggons made their way to the city every Tuesday, and when working, on Saturdays too. Literally dozens of waggons attended the market bringing people, wares and produce from miles around. Some from further afield stayed overnight and returned the following day as their slow speed and lack of sufficient daylight precluded their return the same day. Other markets, for example at Devizes, were also the focal points of their own outlying communities and were serviced in the same way by local carriers.

Carrier's waggons also went much further afield, both to London and across country on fixed or semi-fixed routes where they had developed trade. Travel was very slow and involved a number of overnight stays at various inns along the route. The quality of ride and protection from the elements was no better than that of the local waggons and the traveller had to be hardy to undertake such journeys.

For inter-urban and long-distance travel, the stagecoach and mailcoach became available for those who could afford them, as even travelling on the roof didn't come that cheap! Some of the patronage enjoyed by the long-distance waggons transferred to the stagecoaches which afforded quicker and arguably more comfortable travel. These timetabled coaches travelled regularly to and from London, with many routed through Wiltshire finishing along the south coast and into the West Country. They stopped at coaching inns in Amesbury, Devizes, Downton, Hindon, Ludgershall, Marlborough, Mere, Salisbury, Warminster and Wilton, all of which were to become significant towns in the Wilts & Dorset network.

## NOTICE TO PASSENGERS

Whilst our Staff are, as always, instructed to make every effort to avoid early running, the present difficulty in obtaining reliable watches makes it no longer possible to maintain the same high standard of accurate time-keeping as in pre-war days.

To avoid disappointment, passengers should be at their boarding point at least FIVE MINUTES before the advertised time of departure of the bus by which they desire to travel.

One example of the many stagecoaches running through the area during the late 1830s was *The Magnet*, which ran between London and Weymouth via Basingstoke, Whitchurch, Andover, Salisbury, Blandford and Dorchester. Another was *The Swiftsure* whose route was London-Basingstoke-Whitchurch-Andover-Amesbury-Warminster-Bridgwater. Cross-country stagecoaches also provided a valuable service to travellers, among which were those running out of Salisbury to Christchurch, Exeter, Frome, Poole and Southampton.

A number of waggon owners went on to run market-day motorbuses from their villages and with the advent and growth of the railways some of them ran trucks and vans too, which visited railyards to pick up and drop off goods for their customers. Waggons continued to run into Salisbury well into the 20th century from some of the villages, whereas more industrialised parts of the county made the transition much sooner. South Wiltshire was very much an agricultural area whereas West Wiltshire developed into an area of light industry. North Wiltshire underwent a partial transition from being an agricultural area to an industrial area with the arrival of the large Great Western Railway locomotive works at Swindon in 1841.

Salisbury was linked with the rest of the London & South Western Railway network in 1847 with trains travelling to London via Romsey, Southampton and Eastleigh. A further link via Basingstoke and Andover was introduced ten years later, while its connection with the Great Western Railway came in 1848. Further lines in the area were introduced in the 1850s and 1860s. With the advent of the railways, stagecoaches went into sharp decline, but some adapted their businesses to provide feeder services from places not served by rail to an appropriate mainline station until the advent of bus services which took over this role and developed in their own right.

# 2. A PRIVATE VENTURE

The beginnings of a world war must rate among one of the least encouraging backdrops from which to try and start a successful business venture, unless that business is in armaments or uniform clothing. But it was against just such a background that Amesbury entrepreneur Edwin Coombes started his Wilts & Dorset Motor Service between his home town and Salisbury using a locally-built Scout bus during August 1914.

Coombes took a liking to the name 'Wilts & Dorset' after the Salisbury-based Wilts & Dorset Banking Co Ltd was absorbed by Lloyds Bank earlier in the year, and he decided to save the name from disappearing into oblivion by using it for his new bus company. It wasn't long, however, before he was approached by two gentlemen from Worthing with a view to their buying his embryonic business. Messrs Alfred D. Mackenzie (known as Douglas) and Alfred Cannon were both seasoned busmen who had worked together for some years in a variety of roles and were both now senior officials of Worthing & District Motor Services Ltd. They, together with their associate Percy Lephard, duly purchased the operation from Mr Coombes and registered it at the end of the year as Wilts & Dorset Motor Services Ltd. The company was incorporated from 4 January 1915 with a registered office in Amesbury. Percy Lephard was appointed company chairman, Douglas Mackenzie became secretary, Alfred Cannon a director and Edwin Coombes was retained as manager.

1915 was a busy year for Mackenzie and Cannon. Not only were they establishing Wilts & Dorset, they were also overseeing the amalgamation of three companies, including their own Worthing & District, into the newly-created Southdown Motor Services Ltd. Cannon was appointed managing director of Southdown, while his colleague Mackenzie took the role of director and traffic manager. Their office was based along Marine Parade, Worthing and it was from here that they also directed Wilts & Dorset in the early years. However there was no financial connection between the two companies; Wilts & Dorset was a private venture of Mackenzie and Cannon. Inevitably, however, there were strong visual similarities between the two companies, including vehicles, fleetnumber positions and livery styles together with fleetname, destination board and ticket styles.

The first new bus, a 31-seat Scout, was delivered in December 1914 followed by a further four Scouts during 1915. Three of these had secondhand bus bodies fitted at Worthing, while two were bodied locally by Marks of Wilton. One received a charabanc body, the other was finished as a 31-seat bus.

Scout was a local Salisbury firm who built small quantities of both cars and commercial vehicles, including buses. Apart from Wilts & Dorset, Scout supplied buses to a number of small operators in the area until it ceased production in 1921.

During December 1914, the original Amesbury-Salisbury service was extended to Bulford and Larkhill, beginning the company's long association with the military on Salisbury Plain. It was worked by one of the new Scouts together with a Daimler hired from Worthing Motor Services. At the same time, the original Scout used by Coombes on his Amesbury service was outstationed in Cranborne and ran services into Southampton and Bournemouth. In March 1915, the first of many acquisitions took place when A. A. Brewer of Ringwood was taken over together with his services to Southampton and Salisbury and his Scout single-decker.

August 1916 saw a further new vehicle in the shape of a McCurd single-decker. This was the first Wilts & Dorset vehicle to be painted red — the Scouts ran in a yellow livery. At this time five vehicles were based at Amesbury, one at Cranborne and one at Ringwood.

The company's registered office moved from Amesbury in February 1917 to 2 St Thomas Square, Salisbury, the office of another of the company's directors,

Fh 6242

WILTS & DORSET
Motor Services Ltd.

Issued subject to Regulations in Time Table. This Ticket to be shown on demand.

NOT TRANSFERABLE

SINGLE

Mr G. H. Davis, who later became company secretary. The same year also saw Coombes called-up for military service.

However, clouds were gathering on the company's horizon. A shortage of drivers as the war continued meant that W&D had to suspend all its services with the exception of the Amesbury route and as a consequence put all its Scout vehicles up for sale. One of these was sold to Southdown and by 1918 just the McCurd remained, running the Amesbury route single-handed. Fortunately Wilts & Dorset managed to stay afloat with just one bus on one route, although it would have been all too easy for the company to have slipped into oblivion and become just another casualty of war. Once hostilities ceased, W&D wasted no time in rebuilding its fleet and starting new services. The centre of operations was also switched from Amesbury to Salisbury, with Amesbury remaining as an outstation. A small garage and workshop was constructed in Castle Street, Salisbury, which, as we shall see, was enlarged in later years as the fleet grew and as the company acquired adjoining properties for expansion.

Two AEC YCs and a Leyland S5 entered service during 1919. One of the AECs together with the Leyland had double-deck bodies built by Brush and Dodson respectively, while the remaining AEC was fitted with a charabanc body. The double-deckers were put to work on a new Salisbury city service between St Marks Church and Wilton which started in September 1919, while the charabanc was

used for excursions to places of interest in the area, including Stonehenge.

The following year was certainly an eventful one and saw more new vehicles arrive, more new services start and the arrival of Raymond I. H. Longman, a man destined to become a key figure with W&D for many years to come. It was also a year of stiff competition for the company from its former founder and manager, Edwin Coombes, who had been denied his former position after he was discharged from the Army. 1920 also saw the company change its financial structure from a private limited company to a public limited company in order to provide Wilts & Dorset with the funding it required to pursue its ongoing programme of development and expansion to become a major operator. Five new vehicles joined the fleet during the year, a pair of Dodson-bodied AEC YC single-deckers, a Harrington-bodied Leyland S5 charabanc, an AEC YC double-decker and a small Maxwell 16-seat charabanc.

As yet, Wilts & Dorset had no significant engineering facilities of its own and vehicles requiring overhaul were sent to Southdown's workshops at Brighton until the company later built its own facilities in Salisbury.

A feature of W&D, as with many other operators at the time, was the practice of body swapping between chassis, not just once, but in some cases several times. To give an example, AEC YC no7 (CD 3330), was delivered with a Harrington 31-seat charabanc body in June 1919.

About to leave Salisbury on the local service out to Wilton is 13 (CD 5249), a Dodson-bodied AEC YC new in May 1920. This bus was rebodied as a single-decker in 1923 and was withdrawn in October 1929. *Phil Davies Collection*

▲ During 1921 this was exchanged for a Dodson double-deck body and four years later it was given a 31-seat Harrington single-deck body before being withdrawn in 1929. It was likely therefore that a chassis with a particular registration number could be seen over a period of time in various guises which can cause headaches for historians trying to compile accurate fleet histories! W&D, however, allocated each body a unique body number so that it knew which bodies the various chassis were carrying.

A further new Salisbury city service to Wilton from Harnham Bridge began in 1920, together with a new long-distance service from Salisbury to Bournemouth via Fordingbridge and Ringwood which it ran jointly with Bournemouth & District Motor Services, renamed Hants & Dorset Motor Services during July. A further new service was introduced between Salisbury and Trowbridge via Warminster, but two years later terminated at Warminster before being discontinued in 1923.

But with expansion came competition, as already mentioned, from Edwin Coombes who was attempting to

re-establish himself with his new company, Salisbury & District Motor Services, also known locally as Yellow Victory, as a serious alternative to Wilts & Dorset. From March 1920 his yellow vehicles plied along each W&D route in an attempt to abstract as many passengers from them as possible to the detriment of his former employer. This was, perhaps, the understandable move of an aggrieved man in the light of his treatment by W&D. Intense competition ensued until August 1921 when Coombes sold his business and nine vehicles to Wilts & Dorset. His fleet comprised seven Thornycroft Js and a couple of Crossley 14-seat charabancs. Two of the Thornycrofts carried single-deck bodies, a further pair were double-deckers which had been used in competition on the Wilton routes and the remaining three were 28/33-seat charabancs. The only new vehicles purchased that year by W&D were a pair of Leyland G3s, one a saloon and the other a double-decker, both with bodies by Leyland. A new service to start in 1921 was that between Salisbury and Southampton via Whiteparish, forging a link with another major centre in the area.

Services listed in the October 1922 timetable show routes radiating from Salisbury to Amesbury, Stonehenge and Larkhill (Service 1); Fordingbridge, Ringwood and Bournemouth (Service 3); Alderbury, Whiteparish and Southampton (Service 4); Codford and Warminster

Leyland G7 27 (HR 9541) is seen on Salisbury City service 2 to Wilton. Delivered in October 1923 with a Harrington 51-seat body, it was rebodied as a charabanc in June 1929 and withdrawn November 1933. *Author's Collection/Pamlin Prints*

(Service 5); Fovant (Service 9); and to Porton (un-numbered). In addition the city services from St Marks Church/Harnham Bridge to Wilton/Ditchampton were numbered 2/2A and several services from Codford were listed, to Salisbury (5A), Frome (5B) and Devizes (5C).

Just one new vehicle came in 1922, a Leyland G7 with a Harrington 26-seat charabanc body. The following year also saw the solitary purchase of a further Leyland G7, also bodied by Harrington, but this time as a double-decker for Salisbury city services.

Mr Longman was appointed company secretary during 1924, the same year that W&D received its first new vehicle on pneumatic tyres, an AEC two-tonner with a Harrington charabanc body, delivered in June. It had been preceded three months earlier by a Harrington-bodied Leyland G7 charabanc on solid tyres. Two more AEC two-tonners on pneumatics joined the fleet in March 1925, with United 24-seat single-deck coachwork, followed in September by W&D's first forward-control bus, a Dodson-bodied Leyland SG11 36-seat single-decker which was used on the Salisbury-Bournemouth service.

A further three properties were acquired in Castle Street, Salisbury, during 1926 in readiness for expansion of existing facilities. In the meantime one of these was put to use as a tyre store. New vehicles consisted of three Leyland G7s, all with Harrington bodies, two finished as charabancs while the third was a further double-decker for Salisbury city services.

1927 was another of those landmark years in Wilts & Dorset's history. Its portfolio of services was steadily growing and in May the company reached Andover by extending its service from Salisbury to Tidworth on to the Hampshire town. Interestingly, it was at Andover that W&D vehicles first met those of Venture, which would later become part of the company. Between Tidworth and Andover, Wilts & Dorset ran in competition with established operator Tidworth Motor Services until April 1929 when that concern was acquired by W&D. This included the route from Salisbury to Tidworth via Winterbourne Gunner, Idmiston, Allington, Cholderton and Shipton Bellinger. During April 1927, B&C Motor Services (Bannister & Corp) was acquired for its Salisbury-Amesbury-Bulford Camp-Tidworth service which strengthened the company's presence on services to and

Brand-new Leyland G3 16 (HR 4483) poses for the camera, complete with boards for service 2A, Harnham Bridge-Salisbury-Wilton. It was new in May 1921 with a Leyland 45-seat body and saw nine years on Salisbury City services before being withdrawn in March 1930. Notice the driver's windscreen and the Hackney Carriage lettering above the registration number. *Phil Davies Collection*

from the camps. W&D, however, had no spare vehicles to use on the service and took the necessary but unusual step of hiring B&C's Guy buses to maintain the service until sufficient company vehicles became available to replace them. Arthur Corp took employment with W&D and was later appointed traffic superintendent at Andover.

Wilts & Dorset once again attracted competition on its Salisbury city routes, this time from Sparrow & Vincent who traded as Victory Motor Services. They launched a concerted attack on the company's Wilton route, and soon expanded to other city services. The small town of Pewsey hosted a new W&D outstation when it provided vehicles for the newly-introduced Salisbury-Amesbury-Marlborough service from November. Pewsey's status, as we shall see later, grew in importance from an outstation to a company depot.

Thirteen new vehicles were delivered during 1927, the largest intake in a single year thus far. Eight were small capacity 19-seat Dennises bodied by Short, the company's first one-man operated buses. These versatile little buses were known as 'chasers' and were used in a variety of roles, such as duplicating high-density services, running quiet rural routes and protecting the company's revenue on services where competitors were also running. A pair of Leyland's recently-introduced PLSC1 Lion chassis with Leyland 31-seat bus bodies arrived in July and were followed later in the year by a further three larger Lion PLSC3 single-deckers with Leyland 36-seat coachwork. The Lions were the first new buses delivered with roller destination displays, replacing the portable route and number boards carried on the front and sides of earlier vehicles.

More property was purchased in Castle Street during 1928, this time on the opposite side of the road, and was put to use as a garage and paintshop.

Further routes had been introduced and by April an impressive list of services appeared in the timetable. Six city services now ran in Salisbury, with country routes radiating to Larkhill, Durrington, Tidworth, Marlborough, Shrewton, Andover, Romsey, Bournemouth, Southampton, Woodfalls, Porton Camp, Coombe Bissett and Shaftesbury.

It is true to say that although the company had a number of outstations designed to reduce dead mileage to a minimum and provide for efficient scheduling by basing both crews and vehicles where they were needed, the whole network at this time was still essentially Salisbury-based.

In terms of new vehicles 11 single-deckers of Dennis and Leyland manufacture arrived in 1928, together with a small 18-seat Dennis coach which featured a canvas-roofed 'all weather' body by Harrington. There were three more small Dennis chasers with 18-seat Short bodies and eight Leyland Lion PLSC3s with a mix of 32- and 36-seat Leyland bodies.

With its programme of continuing service development gaining ever more momentum, Wilts & Dorset found itself with a temporary shortage of sufficient vehicles but managed to fill the gap from surplus Southdown stock. Seven Daimlers of 1919-21 vintage were acquired, six of which entered service. All but one were Dodson-bodied single-deckers, the remaining vehicle carrying a Harrington double-deck body. These were used for between a year and 18 months before being replaced by new vehicles and sold.

Further new vehicles arrived in 1929, new services were started and a new base at Andover was established. It was also the year that Raymond Longman was appointed to the board and became a director of W&D. The company's long association with Endless Street, Salisbury also began with the purchase of No 6 which was used as W&D's traffic office and as a waiting room for passengers.

The new services comprised those out of Fordingbridge to Rockbourne and Breamore, together with two new routes out of Salisbury to Netherhampton and Weymouth. It was Andover, however, which was the new jewel in W&D's crown with three new local town services and a route to Marlborough being introduced.

Leyland provided Wilts & Dorset with all its new vehicles for 1929, starting with three more PLSC Lions with Leyland's own 36-seat saloon bodywork in March. June saw a single example of Leyland's new Tiger TS1 fitted with coachwork by Harrington join the coach fleet. It featured a canvas hood and had seating for 32 passengers. Leyland's new LT series Lion (which superseded the PLSCs), was also represented, with three LT1 single-deckers with 31-seat bodies by Leyland arriving in June and a further four in November.

Perhaps the most important vehicles of the decade came during December 1929, the first fully enclosed double-deckers. Up to now, hapless double-deck passengers had to endure exposure to the elements on an upper deck reached by an exposed staircase. Their plight was similar to 'outside' stagecoach passengers who decades earlier were subjected to similar travelling conditions. Although travel on a warm, sunny summer's day would have been extremely pleasant, travel in wet, cold and windy weather, particularly in winter with bitingly low temperatures and possibly during snowstorms, must have been an endurance for even the most hardy traveller. These new double-deckers were a pair of Leyland Titan TD1s with Leyland lowbridge 48-seat bodies. Low height was achieved by means of a sunken gangway along the offside of the upper deck and Wilts & Dorset specified this type of double-decker until the advent of the Bristol Lodekka in the early 1950s. These were much more versatile than the highbridge type of vehicle, around a foot higher to accommodate a central upper-deck gangway and severely restricted in their route availability.

Three elderly vehicles acquired with the business of Tidworth Motor Services, mentioned earlier in this chapter, consisted of a pair of Leyland Ms, a charabanc and a saloon, and a Leyland C charabanc. The Leyland M's charabanc body was replaced by a Dodson 32-seat saloon body from a withdrawn AEC YC in December and remained in service for a couple of years before being converted into a company lorry which was used until 1948. The remaining two vehicles were withdrawn shortly after acquisition.

1930 was W&D's last year of independence and in June a new service between Andover and Newbury was started in direct competition with L. A. Horne of Andover until the latter capitulated and left the route in sole charge of W&D. Andover & District Motor Services was also acquired in June, together with three vehicles and services between Andover, Romsey and Salisbury which increased the company's presence in the Andover area. A further new W&D service was introduced from Andover to Devizes.

Such was the company's growth, that it opened a new depot in Junction Road, Andover during 1930, which was completed the following year. Another service to make a welcome reappearance in the timetable was that between Salisbury and Trowbridge, which had been withdrawn several years earlier.

Seventeen new vehicles, once again all from Leyland, started to join the fleet from the beginning of the year. First to enter service in January and February were a trio of Leyland Lion LT2s with Leyland 35-seat bodies. A further pair of Leyland-bodied Titan TD1 double-deckers arrived in April, followed in May by four LT2 coaches carrying Harrington 32-seat coachwork. Two further coaches on Tiger TS1 chassis joined the fleet in June, this time bodied by Heaver with seating for 32 passengers. Four more Titan TD1 double-deckers arrived during June and July and the year's intake concluded in August with a pair of 35-seat LT2 saloons bodied by Leyland.

The June takeover of Andover & District produced three small vehicles, a 14-seat Chevrolet, a 20-seat Dennis G and a 20-seat Guy ONDF. The Chevrolet was sold the following month but the other two saw service with W&D for a few more years.

◄ Another rebodied Leyland Tiger TS1 is 85 (MW 6293), new in June 1930, but with its 32-seat Harrington coach body dating from January 1938. The vehicle was rebuilt as shown here by Wilts & Dorset in June 1945 and was withdrawn eight years later in April 1953. *The Omnibus Society*

◄ Despite its radiator proclaiming that this vehicle is a Leyland Titan, 81 (MW 6289) is in fact a Leyland Lion LT2. New in May 1930, it carries a 30-seat Harrington coach body which was rebuilt by ECW in 1943. It was pictured towards the end of its working life at Salisbury bus station on a short-working of service 1 to Woodford before its withdrawal in November 1952. *Maurice Doggett Collection*

◄ 89 (MW 7050) is a Leyland Titan TD1 with a Leyland lowbridge 48-seat body which was delivered in July 1930. Photographed after an extensive rebuild by ECW in 1945, it received a Gardner 5LW oil engine in place of its petrol unit two years later. It was taken out of service in October 1951. *The Omnibus Society*

# 3. UNDER NEW OWNERSHIP

Pictured in original condition in Salisbury City centre on the local service to West Harnham is Leyland-bodied Leyland Titan TD1, 97 (MW 8754). New in February 1931, it was rebuilt by ECW during 1944 and received a Gardner 5LW oil engine in July 1947. It was withdrawn in October 1951 following more than twenty years of service.
*Maurice Doggett Collection*

▲ During March 1931, Wilts & Dorset ceased to be a fully independent company. It now had representatives of the Southern Railway and the Tilling & British Automobile Traction Company (TBAT) on its board, as between them they had acquired sufficiently significant shareholdings to give them jointly a controlling interest in W&D. Under the terms of the Railways (Road Transport) Act of 1928 the railway companies were empowered to purchase major financial interests in road passenger transport companies and the SR exercised this option with the bus companies throughout its area, including Wilts & Dorset.

TBAT held interests in bus companies up and down the country and was always seeking both new investment and increasing its existing investment where it could. The opportunity to take a major stake in Wilts & Dorset arose when the company increased its share capital at the time of the railway interest and as such joined the TBAT fold. The

shareholding of both organisations increased over the next few years which maintained their control over the company.

From May 1931, W&D timetables carried the strapline 'In association with the Southern Railway' to reflect its new involvement with the railway company. A Standing Joint Committee was set up, consisting of senior officials of both the Southern Railway and Wilts & Dorset which discussed operational matters and policy covering issues of mutual interest to both transport companies. Such matters included road/rail ticket inter-availability, joint ventures such as road/rail excursions, reciprocal publicity and enquiries arrangements, reciprocal rail/road breakdown and emergency cover, rail timetables in W&D timetables, discussions on proposed new and revised bus services and a variety of other matters which arose as part of operational life. Children's fares were also brought into line with those of the SR with under 3s travelling free and those aged between 3 and 14 paying half the adult fare.

An interesting early spin-off from the Southern Railway was the carriage of pastry on Wilts & Dorset buses from June 1931! J. Lyons & Company produced packages of pastry which it then sent by rail to its customers. Pastry for consignees who fell beyond the range of the SR delivery vans continued its journey by bus with Wilts & Dorset receiving 4d (approx 1.6p) per packet for the pleasure.

From minutes of these meetings, it seems that when it came to revenue apportionment on joint operations, the railway came away with the lion's share, leaving Wilts & Dorset a little light in the pocket!

During 1930 and 1931, the works and garage respectively in Castle Street were enlarged and extended to meet the new requirements of a developing and growing company. Indeed, from just one bus at the end of World War 1, the fleet total in 1931 had grown to a very respectable 74 which ran some 2.8 million miles during the year. Vehicles were based at Salisbury, Andover, Bowerchalke, Bulford, Fordingbridge, Larkhill Camp,

Marlborough, Shaftesbury, Tidworth, Whiteparish, Wilton and Woodfalls.

Numerous local operators were acquired during the 1930s and beyond. In most cases Wilts & Dorset acquired just the goodwill and took over the services, but as a matter of policy rarely purchased the vehicles. The more significant of these, and those where vehicles were taken into stock, will be highlighted as the story unfolds. Perhaps surprisingly, the majority of operators taken over, in fact, approached W&D offering themselves for sale rather than the company being on the lookout for the next purchase.

Investment in new vehicles continued during 1931 with a mix of Leyland and Morris vehicles joining the fleet. Nine further Leyland TD1 double-deckers with Leyland bodies were purchased at a cost of £1,657 each together with a further pair of Leyland Tiger TS1 coaches bodied by Harrington. A new departure, however, was the purchase of six Morris Commercial Viceroy single-deckers with 24-seat bodies by Heaver at a cost of £796 each.

Wilts & Dorset's network of services from Andover was enhanced with new service to Hungerford, Broughton and Redenham in 1931. Services were renumbered the following year to tidy up the piecemeal numbering system. Services were broadly grouped in areas, but town and city services were not given route numbers but rather allocated into 'sections'. A couple of new services were proposed,

one from Salisbury to Southsea and the other from Salisbury to Yeovil, but in the event nothing came of either. Another new service from Salisbury to Winchester was also proposed but several years were to elapse before its introduction.

Just seven new vehicles, all coaches, were purchased during 1932, five Leyland Tiger TS3s bodied by Harrington which arrived in April and a further pair of 20-seat Morris Commercial Viceroys, also bodied by Harrington, were delivered during May.

More property was purchased by the company in Castle Street, adjoining the garage on the south side of the street, and during the year land was purchased in Amesbury for a bus station and waiting area which opened during the summer of 1933.

The new vehicle intake for 1933 comprised six Leyland Titan TD2 double-deckers with Leyland 48-seat bodies. These were joined, however, by a mixed bag of 16 vehicles taken over from Sparrow & Vincent of Salisbury's Victory Motor Services. These consisted of five saloons, six coaches, and five charabancs of Albion, Dennis, Daimler, Gilford, Leyland and Reo manufacture but only around half of these remained with W&D after 1935. It will be recalled that Victory had gone into head-to-head competition with Wilts & Dorset on Salisbury city services during 1927 and had continued to be a thorn in the company's side ever since. The purchase was concluded during December and included goodwill, vehicles and Salisbury city services, another service out to East Grimstead, an express service from Salisbury to the racecourse and a selection of excursion and tours licences from Salisbury Market. A measure of the impact that Victory was having on Wilts & Dorset revenue was reflected in the purchase price of £16,000, a great deal of money in 1933.

During the year the pair of dual door Heaver-bodied Leyland Tiger TS1 coaches, dating from 1930, had their canvas roofs replaced by panelling and at the same time received full-length roof-mounted luggage containers. The opportunity was also taken to seal the front door and just retain the rear entrance.

The need for small buses to operate on lightly-used rural services was initially met by small Dennis buses. The next generation comprised Morris Commercial Viceroys as illustrated by No 125 (MW 8984) which carries a Heaver 24-seat body. New in April 1931, this bus later had its seating reduced to 20 and became single-manned. It had a relatively short working life with Wilts & Dorset and was sold to a dealer in May 1943. *The Omnibus Society*

Leyland Tiger TS3 coach 107 (WV 650) shows off the elegant lines of its 32-seat Harrington bodywork which includes curtains, rear mounted luggage rack and a sliding roof. Just visible at the rear is the ladder giving access to the luggage rack. This coach was delivered in April 1932 and retired from service in November 1952.
*The Omnibus Society*

Another view of one of the Willowbrook-rebodied Leyland TD2s depicts 114 (WV 2384), dating from March 1933, which received this replacement body in March 1946. Notice the Wilts & Dorset badge at the top of its 'Cov-Rad' replacement radiator. This bus was taken out of service in September 1954.
*Maurice Doggett Collection*

This Leyland Titan TD2, 113 (WV 2383), started life as an identical sister vehicle to that shown on page 93. This view shows the bus after rebodying by Willowbrook in April 1946 and the fitting of its longer 'Cov-Rad' radiator at the same time. It entered service in January 1933, received a Leyland 8.6 litre oil engine in February 1938, and was withdrawn after 23 years on the road in November 1956.
*Author's Collection*

Wilts & Dorset maintained a history of profitability and a surplus of £6,759 was recorded during 1933 with an annual mileage now just over the three million mark run by 95 vehicles.

Venture of Basingstoke approached the company during 1933 and offered itself for sale, having previously been refused by the Aldershot & District Traction Company. Following consultation with Aldershot & District, Wilts & Dorset made Venture a token offer of £10,000 which was not acceptable to Venture's directors and the matter was not pursued further.

At the start of 1934 Southern National Omnibus Company approached Wilts & Dorset about its service between Salisbury and Weymouth. This had started in 1929 when Southern National had refused an offer to run the service jointly on a 50/50 basis covering vehicles, mileage and receipts. The offer had been refused again in 1930, but now Southern National sought a joint agreement. As Wilts & Dorset had built up the service and

invested in its success, this approach by Southern National was initially rejected, but following negotiations, agreement was reached and the service was now run on a joint footing.

New vehicles started to arrive in May in the shape of a pair of Leyland Titan TD3 double-deckers with Brush 52-seat bodies. These were followed in July by a couple of Harrington-bodied Leyland Tiger TS6 32-seat coaches. Excursions from Salisbury to Southampton Docks to view the ocean liners were popular; as in previous years, passengers were allowed to go aboard the visiting ships and see their luxury for themselves. As operators of the docks, the Southern Railway was able to provide Wilts & Dorset with advance details of ships visiting Southampton. In addition to the traditional selection of excursions and tours in Wiltshire, Hampshire and Dorset for local people, W&D also ran similar combined road/rail excursions in conjunction with the Southern Railway for passengers from London who joined their coaches at Salisbury station.

Destinations included the New Forest and Bournemouth, Stonehenge and Marlborough, and also Cheddar.

An imaginative series of three-day Land Cruises were also proposed by the Southern, aimed at overseas visitors. Wilts & Dorset coaches would meet designated trains from Waterloo at Salisbury station and travel to places of interest in Wiltshire, Hampshire and Dorset with overnight hotel stops before dropping their passengers off again at Salisbury for their return leg to London on the third day. In the event, however, these tours never got off the ground due to a lack of bookings.

By 1935 service numbers had reached 31, which excluded Salisbury city and Andover town services, which remained un-numbered. A schedule of services operating in October appears in Appendix 1. In common with the previous year's intake, just four new vehicles joined the fleet during 1935, a pair of small Leyland Cub KP3s with Harrington 20-seat coach bodies which arrived in April, and a pair of Leyland Titan TD4 double-deckers with Leyland 52-seat metal-framed bodies delivered three months later. The TD4s were Wilts & Dorset's first vehicles supplied with diesel engines, then known as oil engines. This heralded the start of the company's desire to make the change from petrol to the more economic diesel engine.

Indeed, towards the end of the year two Leyland TD1s dating from 1929 and 1931 received similar Leyland 8.6 litre diesels in place of their petrol engines.

With the increase in the number of vehicles at Andover garage, these premises had been outgrown and were duly extended during the year. By this time around 20 dormy sheds were in use around the network with small numbers of vehicles and crews being strategically placed in outlying areas. An interesting snippet from the company's minute book in November 1935 tells us that the familiar Bisto adverts which were carried on the lower rear panels of double-deckers brought in £7 10s (£7.50) per vehicle per year in revenue. By today's standards it seems paltry, but in 1935 this was quite a respectable sum.

During the year the revenue arrangements on the Salisbury-Bournemouth service were revised by Bournemouth Corporation Transport for Wilts & Dorset vehicles running within the Borough. Up to now a minimum fare was charged as a deterrent to local Bournemouth passengers, with the company retaining any receipts from passengers willing to pay this higher charge. The new arrangements, however, removed the minimum fare and local passengers had to be issued with a special Bell Punch ticket at the prevailing BCT rate for their journey. Tickets were supplied by BCT and carried their

During April 1935, the first pair of 20-seater Leyland Cub coaches with Harrington bodies were delivered to Wilts & Dorset. The second, 120 (WV 7334), is pictured and remained in service until December 1949. *The Transport Museum, Wythall*

overprint, but displayed Hants & Dorset as the operator, due to its heavy involvement in their issue within the Borough. All the revenue from these tickets was paid to BCT and their inspectors were empowered to board Wilts & Dorset buses to ensure that the correct tickets were being issued. Any infringements to these arrangements by either Hants & Dorset or Wilts & Dorset conductors resulted in serious disciplinary measures being handed out to offenders. These measures remained in force until 1970 when normal company tickets could, once again, be issued with an annual payment being made direct to BCT.

A further pair of Leyland TD1s dating from 1929 and 1930 received Leyland oil engines in place of petrol during January 1936. At the same time the canvas-roofed Harrington body of 1929 Leyland Tiger TS1 No 66 was replaced by a new body from the same coachbuilder which featured a panelled roof and a rear roof-mounted luggage container. It was further modernised with a new deeper Tiger radiator. January also saw the first new vehicles of the year arrive at Salisbury. These were a couple of Leyland Tiger TS7 coaches with Harrington 32-seat bodies which continued to follow the recent trend of featuring rear roof-mounted luggage containers. In July two further Leyland Titan TD4s joined the fleet, carrying Leyland 52-seat metal-framed bodies. These, together with all subsequent new

double-deckers, were powered by oil engines. Further small-capacity Leyland Cub coaches were purchased, one delivered in July, the other some four months later in November. These were bodied by Harrington with seating for 20, but did not carry roof-mounted luggage containers.

Further vehicles were acquired with the coaching business of W. Rowland & Sons of Castle Street, Salisbury during October 1936. These consisted of five Leyland coaches dating from 1928 to 1935, together with a couple of ageing charabancs, one a 1924 Leyland and the other a 1912 Rolls-Royce. Three of the coaches survived into the 1950s while the charabancs were gone within a year, the Rolls-Royce fetching £15! Wilts & Dorset took over their excursions and tours licences as well as contract and private hire business.

Another company to offer itself for sale to Wilts & Dorset was Newbury & District. This proposition was considered carefully by the board but the offer was not taken up. This Newbury concern was later acquired by the Thames Valley Traction Company when the Red & White group sold out to the British Transport Commission in 1950.

The Amesbury area came into the spotlight during the year with land being purchased for a new garage in the town and draft plans drawn up by November. This came about, in part at least, because the company was advised that the site on which its garage at Larkhill was situated was now required for development by the School of Artillery and was asked to find an alternative location. After due consideration, it was decided not to relocate at Larkhill but move to Amesbury instead and open a new garage there. It also decided to pull out of the garage at Bulford and transfer its vehicles to Amesbury as this too would save on dead mileage. In Salisbury, further building work was also proposed at the traffic offices in 6 Endless Street by the addition of an extra room.

By the end of 1936 several new services had been introduced, largely as a result of operator acquisitions. These included routes from Devizes to Easterton and Beechingstoke; from Salisbury to Hindon via Tisbury and to Shaftesbury via Hindon, and from Salisbury to Mere.

◀◀ Straight from the factory and looking magnificent is Leyland-bodied, Leyland Titan TD4 141 (WV 7475), which was posed before delivery to Wilts & Dorset in July 1935. It was later rebuilt by Willowbrook during 1947 and gave 22 years of service before being retired in February 1957. *Phil Davies Collection*

◀ In later life, in Tilling-style livery after the war, is all-Leyland Titan TD4 140 (WV 7474) at Salisbury bus station. It joined W&D in July 1935 and was withdrawn in November 1956. *Maurice Doggett Collection*

Another service was that from Tisbury to Newtown.

Leyland, once again, was the sole supplier of the company's new vehicle intake for 1937. First to arrive were the first diesel-engined single-deckers, a pair of Lion LT7s with 32-seat dual-purpose coachwork by Harrington, delivered during March. They had Leyland four-cylinder 5.7litre units. October saw a couple of Titan TD5s with Southdown-style Park Royal 52-seat bodies, concluding ▼ Wilts & Dorset's orders for the year. However, one of the former Rowland Leyland Lion PLSC3s (No 149) dating from 1928 was given a new lease of life when it received a new 32-seat saloon body built at Castle Street works during April.

A new local service in Andover from the Guildhall to Millway Road was added to W&D's growing list of routes, while in Salisbury a new booking office was opened in Blue Boar Row. The new depot in Amesbury opened at the end of September with Larkhall and Bulford garages closing at the same time. Wilton garage was also closed with vehicles operating from Salisbury instead.

Further services came from Bath Tramways and consisted of routes previously run by Lavington & Devizes Motor Services which had recently been taken over by the Tramways company. These included Hindon-Salisbury, Codford-Salisbury, Codford-Warminster plus several journeys between Easterton and Devizes which served primarily to reduce competition and maximise revenue on these routes. The same was true of the purchase of Shergold & White's service between Bulford Camp and Salisbury which was taken over in August at a cost of £1,500.

At the end of 1937 fleet strength was maintained at 100 vehicles, the same as the previous year. A profit of £15,460 was recorded with more than four million miles run and almost 10 million passengers carried. Indeed, so successful was the company that the directors very generously decided to reward all their weekly-paid staff at the end of June with an additional week's pay. This was in addition to the Christmas bonuses which were also paid, and had been for several years past.

A further seven Leyland Titan double-deckers received Leyland 8.6 litre diesel engines the following year. Five of these were TD2s dating from 1933 while the remaining pair were TD3s from 1934. One of the TD2s was re-engined yet again at the end of the year with a Gardner 5LW oil unit, the first of its type in the fleet, at a cost of £320. The Heaver bodies on the pair of Leyland Tiger TS1s delivered in 1930 were removed, sold and replaced with new 32-seat coachwork by Harrington during January. Eight new Leylands arrived during 1938, starting in March with a couple of Lion LT7s with Harrington 32-seat dual-purpose coachwork, followed in June by two Tiger TS8 coaches, again bodied by Harrington with seating for 32 passengers. The same month also saw a pair of Titan TD5 double-deckers join the fleet with a further two arriving the following month, all with Southdown-style Park Royal bodies.

A selection of popular day and half-day excursions ran from Salisbury as in previous years during the summer of

This Leyland Titan TD5, 155 (BAM 51), was photographed before delivery to Wilts & Dorset in October 1937. It had a 52-seat Park Royal body, rebuilt by Portsmouth Aviation during 1947, and remained in service until August 1955.
*Maurice Doggett Collection*

WILTS & DORSET

RELIEF
BHR 740
SAY CWS and SAVE MONEY
Salisbury Co-op

1938. These included trips to such places as Cheddar Caves and Wookey Hole, Weymouth, Southsea, Bournemouth and Sandbanks, Beaulieu Abbey and Lyndhurst, Romsey and Winchester, The New Forest, and Stonehenge. Residents of Amesbury and Andover had smaller programmes which included Weymouth, Southsea, Bournemouth and Sandbanks, plus mystery tours and circular drives.

A proposal was made by Wilts & Dorset to the owner of the Woolpack Inn, next door to their traffic office at 6 Endless Street, Salisbury to exchange premises, whereby W&D would move in to the larger building at No 8. Financial terms were agreed and the move was effected the following year. In the meantime, the sites of 10 Endless Street together with 15/17 Rolleston Street were earmarked for a new bus station in Salisbury which was built during 1939 and opened in August of that year.

Sadly Percy Lephard, director and chairman of Wilts & Dorset since its incorporation in 1915, passed away after a long illness on 27 November 1938. His place as chairman was taken by Mr G. Cardwell, one of the TBAT directors who had joined the board in 1931.

1939 was a year of unprecedented activity and change

for Wilts & Dorset. With war looming, military preparations on Salisbury Plain and around Blandford saw major urgent building projects swing into action very quickly to accommodate vast numbers of service personnel called-up. The 'Peace in our Time' document Chamberlain brought back from Hitler fooled nobody and multiple plans were hurriedly drawn up for large-scale training facilities and barracks to prepare and mobilise our war machine. The huge and intense building programme at Blandford was carried out by Sir Lindsay Parkinson & Co and from the end of May brought numerous buses under contract from a large radius taking workmen to and from the site. Indeed, at its peak, some 119 vehicles were running to and from the Blandford site. One of the main building contractors on Salisbury Plain was W. E. Chivers & Sons which also contracted large numbers of buses for their workmen. Wilts & Dorset was heavily involved in these contracts and amassed some 115 secondhand buses (94 double-deckers and 21 saloons) from a number of operators between April and July to meet demand both for Blandford and Salisbury Plain sites. Half came from Southdown. There were 85 Leyland Titan TD1s from Hants & Dorset, Eastern National, Maidstone & District, Chatham & District, Bolton Corporation, Ribble, Tyneside Tramways & Tramroads Co and Birkenhead Corporation as well as Southdown. Other vehicles included Leyland Lion PLSC3s from Hants & Dorset, AEC Regents from Brighton, Hove & District, Nottingham City Transport and Huddersfield Corporation and Thornycroft and Tilling-Stevens saloons from Southdown. Many were pressed straight into service and ran in the liveries of their previous owners.

As already mentioned, W&D's own double-deck fleet was made up entirely of lowbridge vehicles. However, a significant number of the secondhand double-deckers were highbridge and required very careful routeing to avoid collision damage with the many low bridges, trees etc in the areas concerned. Nonetheless, one of the former Southdown TD1s was written off towards the end of the year when it hit a low bridge. In just a few short months fleet strength had more than doubled but as some of these buses, including all the secondhand single-deckers, had

◀ Resting between duties is Park Royal-bodied Leyland TD5 162 (BHR 740), showing the modifications received during its rebuild by W&D during 1947. This bus joined the fleet in June 1938 and left in January 1956. *Photobus/P. Sykes*

During 1939, 85 secondhand Leyland Titan TD1s were acquired from a number of operators to fulfil contracts to transport workers to and from military construction sites across Salisbury Plain and at Blandford. The arrival of these and other secondhand buses doubled the W&D fleet. One of the 41 TD1s purchased from Southdown was 237 (UF 7403).
It arrived with a Short highbridge body which was replaced by this Willowbrook lowbridge body during 1944. It received a Gardner 5LW oil engine in November 1948, replacing its Leyland petrol unit. Seen on Salisbury City service 60 to Wilton, this bus remained in the fleet until October 1953.
*Phil Davies Collection/Surfleet*

▼ Pictured at Bournemouth bus station in June 1948 is former Southdown Leyland Titan TD1, 23 (UF 7410). It was acquired with a large batch of Titans purchased from Southdown during 1939 for contract work and originally carried a Short highbridge body. This was replaced by the ECW body illustrated in September 1941 and at the same time received its longer radiator. A Gardner 5LW oil engine was installed three months later to replace its petrol unit. This bus remained in service until November 1952. *A. B. Cross*

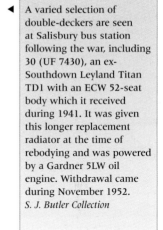

A varied selection of double-deckers are seen at Salisbury bus station following the war, including 30 (UF 7430), an ex-Southdown Leyland Titan TD1 with an ECW 52-seat body which it received during 1941. It was given this longer replacement radiator at the time of rebodying and was powered by a Gardner 5LW oil engine. Withdrawal came during November 1952.
*S. J. Butler Collection*

This final view of one of the numerous secondhand Leyland Titan TD1s is a former Southdown example, 232 (UF 7387), built in 1931 and photographed at Salisbury. It was fitted with this Northern Counties utility body in 1944 and remained in the fleet until January 1952.
*Maurice Doggett Collection/ Surfleet*

The penultimate Leyland Titan to enter service with Wilts & Dorset was this TD5 with Park Royal coachwork, delivered in June 1939, shortly before the outbreak of war. 166 (BWV 663) looks splendid in the prewar red and cream double-deck livery which gave way to Tilling red with cream bands following the end of hostilities. This vehicle gave 17 years of service to the company before withdrawal in November 1956.
*The Omnibus Society*

served their purpose at the conclusion or reduction of contract requirements, they were withdrawn leaving the year-end total at 199, including new vehicles received during 1939.

As with previous orders these were all Leylands and brought three further Titan TD5s with double-deck Park Royal bodies into the fleet in June. Four Lion LT8s and four Tiger TS8s with Harrington dual-purpose 32-seat bodies came during May and June. Four more identical Tigers joined the fleet during December.

New bus services in the Blandford area were developed as a result of the large military presence and the company purchased a plot of land in Salisbury Road to build a new depot. Meanwhile, in Castle Street, the main garage was considerably extended as were the workshops, but half of the property was commandeered by the government for aircraft manufacture the following year, which significantly diminished the space available to W&D to carry out its own maintenance. Despite this, an amazing

amount of vehicle rebuilding was achieved, a real tribute to the professionalism and dedication of the staff concerned.

The recently acquired booking office in Blue Boar Row, Salisbury was loaned to Salisbury Corporation for use by the ARP for the duration of the war. Proposals were also made to extend the recently-opened depot at Amesbury as it was already too small to cope with its extra allocation of vehicles. Cutbacks to normal services took place towards the end of the year as fuel rationing was introduced and in November the first vehicle to be converted to run on producer gas was Leyland Lion LT2 No 91. It had its rear seat removed and an on-board gas producer unit installed. It was a regular performer on services out of Salisbury to Trowbridge and Ringwood until it was converted back to petrol in October 1942. Other vehicles entering the workshops were six Leyland Lion LT1s dating from 1929/30 which were fitted out as ambulances for wartime use before being rebodied after hostilities had ended.

More than five million miles were run during 1939 with more than 13 million passengers carried, yielding a profit of £12,409.

The new decade saw new vehicles arrive, this time consisting of a dozen Bristol K5Gs with Eastern Coach Works 52-seat double-deck bodies which were delivered in January. These cost £1,740 each and were the first chassis

With Leyland purchases drawing to a close, the final batch of new Leylands, some 16 in total, were delivered to Wilts & Dorset between May 1939 and March 1940. The first arrival was 172 (BWV 669), a Tiger TS8 with Harrington 32-seat dual-purpose coachwork. This was rebuilt by Portsmouth Aviation during 1950, with withdrawal following six years later.
*Maurice Doggett Collection*

This Leyland Tiger TS8 179 (CHR 478) with Harrington dual-purpose bodywork entered service in December 1939 and was rebuilt to the condition illustrated by Portsmouth Aviation during 1949. The staff in the background are highly amused by the photographer's endeavours to capture this vehicle on film before it set out on the Andover-Romsey service 83!
*Author's Collection*

▲ and bodies of their type to enter service with W&D. They were joined by eight Leyland Tiger TS8s with Harrington 32-seat dual-purpose bodies which were built in January and March. These were to be the last new Leylands as, following the war, Bristol/ECW became the company's standard suppliers rather than Leyland, Park Royal and Harrington.

During April the registered office moved from St Thomas Square, Salisbury to 8 Endless Street, which now also included the traffic office formerly next door at No 6. By August, the steel framework for the new depot at Blandford had been erected but work was progressing slowly due to difficulties in obtaining materials. By the end of the year fleet strength had dropped to 180 and mileage was down to 4.5 million. Passenger figures, however, now reached almost 15 million and a £13,000 profit was declared.

No new vehicles arrived during 1941, but a dozen of the secondhand Titan TD1s had their chassis renovated and received new lowbridge bodies. Seven of the former

Southdown TD1s were rebodied by ECW while two each received new Wilts & Dorset and Park Royal bodies. The remaining TD1, an ex-Hants & Dorset example, also received a new Park Royal body. Eight of the Southdown TD1s together with the Hants & Dorset vehicle also received Gardner 5LW oil engines in place of their petrol units.

Despite W&D's very heavy commitments and the difficulty in obtaining new vehicles, the Air Ministry still requisitioned nine saloons for its own use. These comprised six Leyland Lion PLSCs, and single examples of a Dennis Arrow, an Albion and a Morris Commercial Viceroy.

The new Blandford depot was finally completed at the end of the summer, the protracted building time being due to difficulty in obtaining building supplies coupled with an initial refusal to grant planning permission by Blandford Town Council which was subsequently overturned on appeal to government.

As a prelude to a major change in TBAT's shareholding arrangements, control of Wilts & Dorset's bus advertising was passed to the publicity department of the Tilling Association when the contract with the Salisbury Billposting Company finished at the end of the year.

During 1942, Tilling & British Automobile Traction decided that their partnership should be dissolved so that each could pursue its own interests within the industry. Accordingly, each TBAT subsidiary was allocated to either British Electric Traction (BET) or to Tilling and Wilts & Dorset was placed under Thomas Tilling Ltd control in September with an appropriate share transfer taking place. Its direction thereafter followed Tilling policies and practices, destined to take the group on a very different path from its BET cousins. Mr Longman's position with Wilts & Dorset undertook two new changes in rapid succession. For many years he had been director and secretary, but from March he was appointed director and general manager. With the allocation of Wilts & Dorset to Tilling, Mr Longman was appointed to the executive staff of Thomas Tilling Ltd from November but still retained his position as director and general manager of W&D as an official of Tilling.

The board were advised at their July meeting that the company had been allocated 10 trailer-type gas-producer plants at a cost of £855 to help conserve the nation's petrol supplies and in readiness for their use erected a gas-producer equipment store in Castle Street, Salisbury.

Once again, no new vehicles joined the fleet during the year but, as before, several reconditioned TD1s from the ranks of the secondhand fleet were given new lowbridge bodies and a new lease of life. One of the former Hants & Dorset Titans was rebodied by the company's Castle Street workshops, while Duple bodied two further ex-H&D, one ex-Tyneside and one ex-Southdown Titan, each at a cost of £950. A further eight Gardner 5LW oil engines were fitted to the secondhand Titans; these were now more expensive, at £450 each.

Additional services operating by the end of 1942 included Salisbury-Tisbury-Shaftesbury (Service 35), Salisbury-Hindon-Mere (37), Salisbury-Winterslow direct (38), Salisbury-Winterslow via Farley (39), Andover-Devizes (40), Salisbury-Devizes (41) and Blandford Market to Blandford Camp. Once again, many of these came via acquisitions which enabled the company to extend or revise some of its existing services as well as introduce new ones.

From the early months of the war the shortage of manpower was making itself felt and conductresses were employed, initially at Salisbury, to help the company maintain its services during these difficult times. However, more were required and the December 1942 timetable carried a company advert seeking young ladies aged between 21 and 40 to apply for work as bus conductors which brought a favourable response.

By the year end some 5.5 million miles had been run and a record 23.6 million passengers carried.

Nine Leyland Titan double-deckers were converted during 1943 for use with the gas producer trailers, with one trailer retained as a spare. These comprised five of Wilts & Dorset's own TD1 and TD2s (Nos 88, 90, 94, 103 and 109) together with one of the rebodied ex-H&D vehicles (No 38) and three of the rebodied former Southdown TD1s (Nos 16, 231 and 235). Initially they were used on a variety of services including the Salisbury-

Bournemouth route but heavy loads, gradients and a lack of suitable pulling power made the company re-evaluate their use. They decided to place them all on to Salisbury city services and used them on the Wilton services where an extra five minutes' running time was added to the timetable. In addition, a special roster of selected drivers was drawn up and the reliability, timekeeping and performance of these vehicles was improved as a result. This arrangement continued until 1944 when petrol was in better supply and the Titans reverted to petrol.

Four new Daimler CWG5 double-deckers with Brush 55-seat utility lowbridge bodies were allocated by the Ministry of War Transport during 1943. They arrived between March and July and unlike their Leyland and Bristol counterparts were fitted with preselective gearboxes rather than the more usual crash boxes. These were placed at Blandford depot and spent their early years on the Salisbury-Blandford-Weymouth service. Interestingly, W&D had applied for a dozen Guy Arab double-deckers but received the Daimlers instead. A new service to run from

Another of the first batch of Bristol K5Gs was ECW-bodied 196 (CHR 495) which arrived during the first months of the war in January 1940. It was rebuilt by W&D during 1954 and is screened-up for duty on Salisbury City Service 51. It retired from service in October 1958. *Maurice Doggett Collection/Surfleet*

Pictured in unbroken grey livery with wartime white markings is Daimler CWG5 261 (CWV 779) with Brush 55-seat utility bodywork, which entered service in March 1943. It was rebuilt twice by Wilts & Dorset, in June 1945 and April 1949, and remained in traffic until October 1957.
*A. B. Cross*

A later view of 261 (CWV 779) shows it in standard W&D livery following its 1949 rebuild. It is seen at Southampton bus station before return to Salisbury on service 37.
*The Transport Museum, Wythall/B. J. Walters*

Blandford from November operated between the Market and Tarrant Rushton RAF Station.

To assist W&D with further much needed vehicles, four AEC double-deckers came on hire from London Transport from January 1943 at a cost of £25 per vehicle per month and remained in service until the following year.

During 1943 the W&D workshops were busily engaged on body rebuilds to five Titan TD1s and a Lion LT8 with other body rebuilds being carried out by ECW to a Lion LT1 and four LT2s. Several more secondhand Titan TD1s were given new bodies. Of the former H&D vehicles, two were rebodied by ECW and one by Duple, while single examples of former Tyneside TD1s were bodied by ECW and Duple. Concluding the year's programme an ex-Southdown TD1 was rebodied by Willowbrook and Gardner 5LW oil engines were fitted to four of the secondhand TD1s.

A further approach was made by Newbury & District in an attempt to persuade Wilts & Dorset to buy it. Once again, this was carefully considered by the board but rejected due to the high price sought for the company's goodwill.

From 1944 the pace of chassis renovations, body rebuilds and rebodyings really took off. The company's own workshops rebuilt seven Leyland Lions and Tigers and a Leyland Titan as well as completely rebodying a pair of Titans. ECW also carried out extensive rebuilds to seven Titan TD1s as well as rebodying three of the secondhand Titans. Further secondhand Titans were rebodied by Willowbrook (three), Brush (six) and Northern Coach Builders (seven). One of the ex-H&D Titan TD1s (No40), which had received a new Duple body during 1942, was burnt out in December due to a tyre overheating while working in service between Salisbury and Amesbury. Rather than scrap the vehicle, it was decided to give it another new body which was built by Northern Coach Builders in 1946.

A new depot was established at Frog Meadow, Pewsey, at the end of the year, following the acquisition of the excursions and tours licences and the stage service licence between Pewsey and Hungerford from Lampards Garages. This replaced an outstation which had existed since June 1927.

The year-end statistics revealed that W&D continued to be in a healthy financial position, having carried 24.7 million passengers, run five million miles with 181 vehicles and made a profit of £14,000. Notes in the board minutes report that all W&D's services were heavily laden during the year and that an unprecedented 6,700 miles were lost due to severe fog and frost during December.

January 1945 saw a continuation of severe winter weather conditions, causing almost 11,000 service miles to be lost. The general manager's report of April 1945 states that of a total staff of 726, 155 were conductresses based at Salisbury (74), Andover (39), Amesbury (22), Blandford (11) and Pewsey (9). However, with the war coming to an end in May and with former conductors returning to the company, the number of conductresses began to reduce.

Further rebodyings took place during the year with Beadle providing new bodies for seven Lion PLSC3s, and Wilts & Dorset building new bodies for a pair of 1929 Lion LT1s. The last four secondhand Titan TD1s in the rebodying programme received lowbridge bodies from Willowbrook; 48 out of the 85 acquired TD1s had been given new bodies and a further six had been extensively rebuilt.

Rebuilds carried out by Wilts & Dorset included a couple of Tiger TS1 coaches, a Lion LT1 and a pair of Lion LT7s together with three of the recently-delivered Daimler double-deckers which were brought in for a number of modifications. ECW rebuilt four W&D Titan TD1s and three ex-Ribble examples as well as four Tiger TS3 coaches.

By September 1945 a major revision and renumbering of services had taken place in which route numbers were arranged in geographical blocks which now included Salisbury city and Andover town services. The new series ran from 1 to 83 with gaps for new or revised services. These are listed in Appendix 2.

The first new vehicles for a couple of years and, indeed, the first postwar buses, arrived during March 1946 in the shape of a pair of Bristol K5Gs with ECW 55-seat double-deck bodies. These were followed by a further batch of three K5Gs during May and June. While these buses concluded the new vehicle intake for the year, significant numbers of rebodied and rebuilt vehicles re-entered

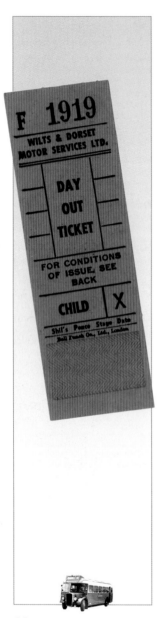

service. Four Lion PLSC3s received new saloon bodies from Beadle, while Willowbrook built new double-deck bodies for four Titan TD2s and a single TD3.

In addition to Wilts & Dorset's own workshops, which rebuilt two Leyland Titan TD5s, comprehensive rebuilds were carried out by outside coachbuilders. Leyland Titan double-deckers were given a new lease of life by ECW (five TD1s together with a TD2 and a TD3), Willowbrook (four TD4s) and Lancashire Aircraft (two TD1s). Rebuilt saloons and coaches comprised a Tiger TS6 and TS7 coach by Portsmouth Aviation and single examples of TS1 and TS6 coaches plus three TS8 coaches by W&D's workshops. The latter also gave a new lease of life to a Lion LT2 saloon. A dozen more Titans received Gardner 5LW oil engines, including a further five of the secondhand TD1s and a single TD2.

Further new services and revisions were introduced during the year, as were the first excursions to operate since before the war. A small number of drivers and vehicles were provided to make a tentative start with a limited programme at Easter, progressively increasing during the summer. Between April and September almost 119,000 excursion miles were run. New services included the 74, a local Andover town service between the Guildhall and King George Road, and the 85 from Salisbury to Amesbury via Everleigh. The number 74 was re-issued following the withdrawal of the Andover-Perham Down service. Others were the 31 from Tisbury to Newtown and the 63, a Salisbury city service from the Market to the Railway Station Yard.

Mr Longman was promoted, once again, in October as managing director of Wilts & Dorset by Thomas Tilling. The premises at 45 Blue Boar Row, Salisbury, were handed back to W&D following war use and the company decided to sell this property as its previous function as a booking office was now carried out at the bus station. Year-end results recorded the highest profit yet, at £29,660. Mileage was also up, at 6.2 million with 186 vehicles, and passenger numbers totalled 22.7 million.

By 1947 things were settling back to normal and with curfews and timing restrictions lifted, services picked up

and development continued. Excursion and private hire business was on the increase and new vehicles were gradually becoming available, albeit in small numbers to start with.

Weekend leave service applications were lodged with the Traffic Commissioners for express services between Bulford Camp and Gloucester via Cheltenham and to Bristol via Bath. These were the start of a number of regular weekend express services for military personnel on Salisbury Plain to various parts of the country. The Salisbury-Whiteparish-Romsey service (35) was extended to Winchester, jointly with Hants & Dorset, and a new service began between Andover and Marlborough (84). Application was also made for a new service between Amesbury and Warminster via Chitterne (23) which started the following year.

Seven new double-deckers arrived between April and December 1947, all Bristol Ks with ECW 55-seat bodywork. Five of these were powered by Gardner five-cylinder 5LW engines, while two were fitted with higher-powered six-cylinder Bristol AVWs. The rebuilding programme was still in full swing, with many more rebuilds being carried out in the company workshops. These comprised some 10 coaches and dual-purpose vehicles made up of Leyland Lions, Tigers and Cubs, together with five more of the secondhand Titan TD1s and a couple of TD5s. Willowbrook was commissioned to rebuild a further Titan TD4, while Portsmouth Aviation rebuilt a pair of Titan TD5s as well as a couple of ex-Rowland Lion coaches and a dual-purpose Tiger TS8. Beadle, once again, received orders to rebody more vehicles, this time six saloon bodies for Lion LT1s. More Gardner 5LW oil engines were fitted in place of petrol engines to a further eight Titan TD1s and a pair of Lion LT2 saloons.

Year-end figures showed a further improvement on those for 1946 with a profit of £31,251 reported. The fleet comprised 191 vehicles which ran 7.4 million miles, including more than 400,000 miles on private hire and excursions. Staffing levels had now reached 913 and passengers carried totalled almost 25 million.

# 4. NATIONALISATION

A new chapter in the history of Wilts & Dorset opened during 1948 when ownership of the company was vested in the British Transport Commission. The BTC had been set up under the Transport Act 1947 by the new Labour Government and took over ownership of railway companies' shares in bus undertakings, which included a significant number held by the Southern Railway in Wilts & Dorset. Tilling Motor Services took the decision to sell its shareholdings in the many bus companies they controlled to the BTC voluntarily. The sale was concluded during November but backdated to 1 January 1948. The remaining private shareholders were bought out by the Government and it is reported that those of W&D received the highest payout per share of the Tilling companies owing to the very healthy financial state of the company.

After the sale of the Tilling Group had been concluded, Mr Longman was appointed as an official of the BTC from December 1948, but remained as managing director of W&D. Mr Cardwell relinquished chairmanship at the beginning of 1948 to take up a new appointment with the Road Transport Executive within the BTC and was replaced by Mr S. Kennedy.

On the service front, applications were made to extend both the Salisbury-Mere and the Salisbury-Shaftesbury services to Yeovil, each of which was granted and began the following year.

Between 1948 and 1954 the rebuild programme continued, albeit on a much-reduced basis, carried out by both W&D and, to a lesser extent, Portsmouth Aviation. During this period many more of the secondhand Leyland TD1s received Gardner 5LW oil engines.

Seven new vehicles arrived in 1948, a pair of Bristol K5Gs each costing £3,025 which arrived in March, three Bristol K6Bs in December, and a couple of Bristol L6B coaches with Beadle 32-seat bodywork also arrived at the end of the year, each costing £2,333. These bodies were virtually identical to those supplied to Southdown on

Leyland Tiger PS1 chassis and were ordered from Beadle due to ECW being unable to supply coach bodies at that time due to the very high demand for new bus bodies after the war.

A further six Beadle-bodied Bristol L6B coaches joined W&D between February and May 1949 together with a single example bodied by Portsmouth Aviation which came in April. These were joined by three Bristol K6Bs in September and a single Bristol K5G in December. An interesting and unique modification was carried out to 1936 Leyland Titan TD4 No145 when it was equipped with fluorescent interior lighting, one of the first installations of

Pictured in pristine condition at Basingstoke is Bristol K5G 282 (EMW 287) dating from March 1948. This bus remained in service until February 1963. *Photobus*

its kind. It was subsequently removed and normal tungsten lighting reinstated.

A new joint service with Hants & Dorset, numbered 68, was introduced towards the end of the year between Andover and Winchester and applications were lodged with the Traffic Commissioners for new express services for service personnel between Boscombe Down and Portsmouth, Bristol, Cheltenham and Oxford. Services to the same destinations from Netheravon and Upavon were also applied for at the same time. A new express feeder service between Ablington and Andover Junction station started during April. A number of other operators also applied for and operated weekend leave express services from Salisbury Plain and generally there was a spirit of co-operation between operators.

From the summer, the well-established service between Salisbury and Trowbridge was run jointly with Western National, which had operated for a number of years along part of the route between Trowbridge and Warminster.

Mr Longman took over the chairmanship of Wilts &

Postwar Bristol L6B coach, 284 (FAM 1), with Beadle 32-seat coachwork is seen laying over at Victoria Coach Station while on express duties to London. Delivered in May 1949, this coach was rebuilt by W&D during late 1956 and taken out of service in September 1962.
*Author's Collection*

Photographed early in its working life at Weymouth before return to Salisbury is Bristol K6B, 287 (FAM 4). Of interest is the full three-piece destination display over the rear platform which was removed during 1953. New in December 1948, this bus gave 16 years' service and was withdrawn in April 1964.
*Maurice Doggett Collection/ A. M. Wright*

Dorset from Mr Kennedy at the start of 1949, giving him the position of Chairman & Managing Director, which he retained for several years to come.

Further applications were lodged with the Traffic Commissioners during 1950 for express services from Amesbury to Bristol and Cheltenham; Blandford Camp to Birmingham and London; Boscombe Down to London; Barton Stacey Camp to Basingstoke and from Bramley Camp to London.

A reintroduction of one-man operation after an absence of several years took place at Pewsey on a number of lightly-used journeys on services 16 and 18 from March 1950. These were worked by a pair of 20-seat Harrington-bodied Leyland Cubs dating from 1936 which had been modified with vacuum door equipment for their new role. These ran for a couple of years before being replaced by a pair of ex-Venture Bedford OBs, also modified with vacuum operated doors and fitted with Perkins diesel engines.

A noteworthy rebuild carried out in the workshops in March involved the fitting of Leyland Lion LT7 154 with a full front in place of its half cab. This made this vehicle unique in the fleet until its withdrawal in February 1956. A large intake of 29 new vehicles was delivered during 1950, including 11 Bristol K5Gs, two KS5Gs and five Bristol KS6Bs all with ECW bodies. The new KS-type was one foot longer than the K-type at 27ft, reflecting revised legislation on vehicle dimensions, but still carried 55 seats, the same as the shorter K. Six Bristol L6Bs with 35-seat ECW bodies and a pair of Bristol LL6Bs with ECW 39-seat bodies made up the saloon arrivals, the newly-introduced LL-type also reflecting revised vehicle dimensions which now allowed two-axle single-deckers to be built to a maximum length of 30ft. The balance of the new arrivals comprised three Bristol L6B coaches with 32-seat Portsmouth Aviation coachwork.

Venture Ltd of Basingstoke had been started during the general strike on 1 May 1926 by a member of the Thornycroft family who, at that time, were prolific manufacturers of bus and lorry chassis in the town. The company developed a number of local town routes as well

as those travelling further afield to such places as Bramley, Andover, Whitchurch, Worting, Alton, Cheriton, Steventon, Baughurst, Winchester, Tadley, Newbury and Aldermaston. Having tried to sell itself to a number of larger operators Venture was acquired by the Red & White United Transport Co Ltd of Chepstow in March 1945. It remained a member of the Red & White Group until 10 February 1950 when that Group's UK bus operations were sold to the BTC. Venture was therefore placed under the control of Wilts & Dorset with vehicles and services still carrying their Venture numbers and running much as before while the company was being integrated with W&D.

This was completed on 1 January 1951 when the Venture services were renumbered by having 100 added to their original numbers and the fleet was renumbered into a new 400/500 series with Wilts & Dorset fleetnames

▲ Preserved 285 (FAM 2) is a Bristol L6B with Beadle 32-seat coachwork. Delivered in May 1949, it carries the attractive maroon, red and cream coach livery introduced in the late 1930s and very similar in style to that carried by Southdown coaches, albeit in green. This coach was photographed at the Stourpaine steam rally during September 1971 and still awaits the application of its fleetnames and fleetnumbers. *Phil Davies*

After an absence of several years, Wilts & Dorset re-introduced one-man operation to selected rural services from Pewsey depot in March 1950. 146 (AHR 521) was one of the pair of small Leyland Cubs with Harrington 20-seat coach bodies which heralded this return.

It was fitted with vacuum-operated door equipment prior to taking up its new role. Delivered in July 1936, it ran for more than two years as a one-man bus before being withdrawn in November 1952. *Maurice Doggett Collection*

Unique in the Wilts & Dorset fleet was 154 (AMW 482), a 1937 Leyland Lion LT7 with Harrington 32-seat coachwork. Originally a half-cab coach, it was extensively rebuilt by W&D in March 1950, at which time it was modified with the full front as shown in this photograph. It gave a further six years' service with the company until its withdrawal in February 1956. *Maurice Doggett Collection*

One of only eight Bristol KS double-deckers to be purchased by W&D was 320 (GMW 851), a KS5G with ECW 55-seat bodywork which entered service in December 1950. It was photographed at Bournemouth bus station, having travelled to the resort as a relief working on service 38. This bus was withdrawn and sold in November 1966. *Bristol Vintage Bus Group*

Venture 38 (COT 551) is a Park Royal-bodied AEC Regal coach which joined the Basingstoke company in May 1938. It passed to Wilts & Dorset in January 1951 with the rest of the Venture fleet and received fleetnumber 438. Its stay was very short-lived; it was withdrawn during the summer. *R. H .G. Simpson*

Another numerically small class of bus to enter service with W&D were three Bristol LL6B 30ft-long saloons, represented here by 321 (GMW 911) which was delivered in January 1951. It had a 39-seat ECW body and remained in service until October 1965. *Bristol Vintage Bus Group*

replacing the Venture name. Forty-six buses and coaches were transferred, all AECs apart from two Bedfords. Of these, 25 were double-deckers, five were saloons and 16 were coaches. Six Guy Arab double-deckers, which effectively entered the Venture fleet between 10 February and 31 December 1950, were transferred to Thames Valley for Newbury & District on 31 December 1950, their place being taken by an AEC Regent from Newbury & District and the allocation to Wilts & Dorset's new Basingstoke depot of one Bristol K (No 290) and four new Bristol KS6Bs (315-8) from 1 January 1951. A couple of former Venture saloon cars, a van, an AEC Regent breakdown lorry and a Thornycroft lorry were also absorbed by W&D at the same time.

Premises acquired comprised the garage and stores in Victoria Street, Basingstoke, the garage at Baughurst which was constructed of wood, the garage at Andover Street, Whitchurch, a piece of outstation land at Tadley and the leased former head office in Wote Street, Basingstoke.

Further express service applications were made for routes between Bulford Camp and Portsmouth, Tidworth to London and Exeter; Barton Stacey to London and Birmingham and from West Down Camp to London.

Nineteen new buses entered service during the year,

a further Bristol LL6B saloon, a further Bristol KS5G double-decker and 17 Bristol KSW5G double-deckers which were built to the new legal maximum width of 8ft instead of the previous 7ft 6 in of the K and KS types.

1952 was an exceptional year for new vehicles with no less than 43. Thirty were Bristol KSW5G double-deckers with ECW 55-seat bodies, while the remaining 13 new arrivals were the first of many underfloor-engined single-deckers to be purchased by W&D, Bristol LS6Gs with dual-door, dual-purpose ECW bodies seating 39. These, together with subsequent twin-door LS vehicles, had the rear door removed and an extra pair of seats fitted during 1955, which made them more suitable for excursion, express and private hire duties. Company staff well remember the twin doors on these vehicles having a mind of their own by opening and closing while in service without any assistance from the crew! These Bristols were delivered in the attractive maroon, cream and red coach livery and when compared with similar vehicles from other Tilling fleets looked particularly splendid. In addition to the new intake, 15 secondhand saloons and coaches from Hants &

▼ Numbered 45 (ECG 646) in the Venture fleet, this AEC Regent with utility 56-seat highbridge Willowbrook bodywork entered service in September 1942. It too was taken over in January 1951 and allocated fleetnumber 445. It continued to give further service for a few more years until withdrawal in August 1954.
*R. H .G. Simpson*

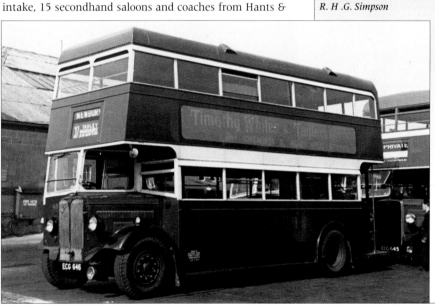

Clearly showing its London ancestry is ex-Venture AEC Regal 412 (UU 6650), new to London General as T35 in 1929. Its 29-seat Chiswick body still features its open platform while in use by Wilts & Dorset. Acquired with the Venture business on 1 January 1951, this bus was withdrawn in October 1953.
*The Transport Museum, Wythall/B. J. Walters*

Wilts & Dorset's Tilling red and cream suits the lines of this AEC Regent very well. Bodied by Lydney to a Weymann design, this highbridge 56-seater dating from 1948 came to Wilts & Dorset from Newbury & District in January 1951 in part-exchange for six Guy Arabs newly delivered to Venture at the time of the takeover. It had a large AEC 9.6 litre diesel engine and pre-selector gearbox, and, following a very respectable 11 years with the company at Basingstoke, 500 (EJB 521), was taken out of service in September 1962.
*Maurice Doggett Collection*

Wilts & Dorset took over control of Venture Ltd of Basingstoke in January 1951 and not only expanded its operating area but also acquired Venture's vehicles. These were predominantly AECs and thereby introduced new types to the company. Pictured at Basingstoke is 483 (FOT 204), an AEC Regal with 35-seat bodywork by Duple. Delivered to Venture during April 1947, this bus remained in service with W&D until September 1961.
*Photobus*

New to Venture in February 1948, 494 (GCG 815) passed to Wilts & Dorset in January 1951. This vehicle is an AEC Regent III with highbridge Lydney body to Weymann design. The roof dome looks a little battered following encounters with low trees. This handsome vehicle remained in service alongside its Bristol stablemates, a couple of which are seen alongside at Basingstoke, until May 1962. *Photobus*

▲ Wearing the much simplified coach livery of cream and red introduced in 1958 is 297 (GAM 216), a Bristol L6B with Portsmouth Aviation 32-seat coachwork dating from January 1950. This coach was withdrawn in January 1962 and was photographed in beautifully restored condition in September 1977. *Mark Hughes*

Fleet replacement continued into 1953 with another bumper intake of new vehicles. These consisted of more of the same, with 23 further dual-door, dual-purpose Bristol LS6Gs and 22 more Bristol KSWs joining the fleet of which 15 were fitted with Bristol six-cylinder AVW engines and seven with the lower-powered Gardner 5LW five-cylinder. The latter vehicles cost £3,733 each. The 15 KSW6Bs were the first W&D double-deckers to be fitted with platform doors and were used on longer-distance services.

A new joint service with Thames Valley, 122, also started in May 1953 linking Basingstoke with Newbury via Kingsclere.

In October 1954 a new bus station and depot was opened in Bridge Street, Andover replacing the previous station built in 1941/42 and vehicle parking area to its rear. The depot was the second in the town and replaced the original building in Junction Road which had become too small and also too costly in terms of local dead mileage. The booking office in the High Street was closed at the same time and a new one opened at the bus station.

The first three of Bristol's new Lodekka double-deckers arrived in March 1954 for Salisbury City services. These 58-seaters with ECW bodies were built to lowbridge dimensions, but due to their low-slung chassis were able to offer highbridge-style upper-deck seating with a central gangway, the first new Wilts & Dorset double-deckers so equipped. A further four Lodekkas joined the fleet at Salisbury between May and October. One of these, 604, travelled to Scotland after completion by ECW at Lowestoft for demonstration purposes to W. Alexander & Sons and to Central SMT before heading south and entering service in Salisbury during late 1954.

A surprising vehicle order called for 15 rear-entrance half-cab Bristol LWLs for rural services. The management considered that some of the rural roads were of such poor quality that their underfloor-engined buses would be damaged and felt that the more robust and higher-sitting LWL would avoid damage and expensive repairs. These buses were specially built by Bristol and ECW and were delivered in October 1954. After only a few years, however, they were rebuilt for one-man operation as described later.

To counteract a shortage of single-deckers, Wilts & Dorset exchanged 10 elderly Leyland Titan TD1 double-deckers for 10 1937 Leyland Tiger TS8s from Crosville in April 1952. The first of these, 506 (BFM 155), with ECW 32-seat bodywork is illustrated, and remained in use for two and a half years until October 1954.
*S. J. Butler Collection*

▲ Dorset and Crosville also joined the fleet for short-term use to ease a shortage of single-deckers pending new deliveries. Those from Hants & Dorset comprised three old Leyland Tiger coaches which had all been withdrawn within 15 months and a couple of ageing Bristol L5G saloons which lasted until the mid-1950s. Ten Leyland Tiger TS7 saloons with ECW 32-seat bodies arrived from Crosville in exchange for the same number of Leyland Titan TD1 double-deckers which were now surplus to requirements, having been replaced by Bristol KSWs. These Tigers remained in service until the latter part of 1954 when they were replaced by new saloons.

Further express services were started to London from Bulford Camp, Larkhill, Perham Down and Tilshead with additional routes opening up the following year to the Midlands and the North.

BOW 169 was purchased from Hants & Dorset as a Beadle-bodied 32-seat saloon in February 1952 and carried fleetnumber 504. Built in 1938, this Bristol L5G, which still retains its prewar-style high radiator, was converted into this breakdown vehicle during January 1956. It was photographed at Basingstoke during the summer of 1971.
*John Hypher*

Bristol LS6G 543 (JMR 639), with ECW dual-purpose 39-seat coachwork, is seen carrying its short-lived experimental coach livery of cream with maroon relief which it wore between November 1957 and August 1958.
*Maurice Doggett Collection/ Surfleet*

A rare photograph showing one of the Bristol LSs with both front and rear entrance/exits still intact. LS6G 545 (JMW 413) was new in July 1953. It lost its rear doorway in February 1955 and gained an extra couple of seats, increasing its capacity to 41.
*Phil Davies Collection*

Bristol KSW5G 338 (HHR 750) picks up at Laverstock Schools as a relief working on Salisbury city service 65 during August 1968. New in December 1951, it survived until December 1969.
*David Gillard*

Bristol KSW5G driver training vehicle 9092 (HMR 59) was a regular service bus for almost 20 years before its conversion and transfer to the service fleet in May 1971. It carried fleet number 344 while in passenger use and was pictured at Basingstoke in its gleaming yellow livery soon after its release from workshops in the summer of 1971. *John Hypher*

Pictured at Basingstoke is Bristol KSW5G 357 (HMR 809) with standard lowbridge ECW bodywork which joined the fleet in April 1952. It was renumbered 367 in September 1971 as part of the fleetwide Hants & Dorset renumbering scheme and was transferred to that company in October 1972 in common with all W&D vehicles still extant at that date. *Photobus*

364 (HWV 293) was photographed on Service 9 at Gomeldon on the Salisbury-Marlborough route during September 1971 on one of its last journeys before withdrawal. Dating from July 1952, this bus was renumbered 373 soon after this photo was taken and withdrawn at the end of the month. *David Mant*

Bristol KSW5G 365 (HWV 294) passes the W&D garage in Castle Street, Salisbury *en route* from Waters Road to the city centre and thence to Bishopdown on service 62 in March 1969. Open platform Lodekka 607 passes in the opposite direction on its way to Waters Road on service 61. The KSW was renumbered 374 in September 1971 and taken out of service the following month. *David Gillard*

Once a familiar sight, but alas no more: a group of Bristol KSW5Gs wait in the sunshine for their next tour of duty at Basingstoke bus station during the autumn of 1971. *John Hypher*

Salisbury yard is the setting for this line up of Bristol KSW5Gs as they stand off-peak ready for afternoon service during March 1971. The staggered seats, a feature of some of these buses, are just visible on the upper deck of the leading vehicle. *David Mant*

48

49

The Bristol Lodekka introduced a standard and versatile lowheight double-decker with a central gangway on the upper deck and a normal two-plus-two seating layout to Tilling group companies during the early 1950s and was appreciated by operators, passengers and staff alike. It also introduced six-cylinder power units to the double-deck fleet rather than the more usual five cylinders specified hitherto. 607 (LMR 740) is a Bristol LD6B with a 58-seat ECW body which joined the fleet in January 1955 and is pictured on local Salisbury city service 57 to Meyrick Avenue. This bus was later renumbered 408 and passed to Hants & Dorset in October 1972. *David Gillard*

The only other arrival that year was a further solitary Bristol LS6G in February.

With the decline in bus patronage beginning to take a firm hold, partly due to a rise in car ownership, and partly due to a much wider availability of television, particularly rental sets, which reduced demand for evening leisure travel, general one-man operation was introduced from 1955/56. The large LS-type buses were used on routes where passenger numbers had dropped significantly and started a trend which gained momentum through the rest of the fifties, sixties and beyond.

Ten more Bristol LD6B Lodekkas arrived for Salisbury City services during 1955 together with 13 Bristol LS5Gs with seating for 41. They had a single front entrance, bus seats and OMO equipment and the five-cylinder Gardner 5HLW engine as they would not be required for the more demanding express and excursion duties. These were the first OMO vehicles, other than the Leyland Cubs and Bedford OBs at Pewsey, to be operated by Wilts & Dorset since before the war. Two of them replaced the Bedfords, while the others entered service from Andover and Basingstoke.

The double-deck fleet wore a standard livery of Tilling red with a couple of cream bands, and the single-deck front-engined buses largely followed the same principle, albeit with a single cream band. The underfloor-engined

1954 Bristol LWL5G 565 (LAM 745), with rear-entrance 39-seat bodywork is pictured at Salisbury in original condition.

The same vehicle, photographed at Salisbury in July 1963, is seen in its rebuilt condition following its conversion for one-man operation by Wilts & Dorset in April 1959.
*Maurice Doggett Collection/ Maurice Doggett*

Bristol LWL5G 557 (LAM 107) is parked alongside a similar vehicle, at Salisbury bus station in August 1962. Delivered during October 1954 as a standard half-cab bus with ECW rear-entrance bodywork, these LWLs were modified as shown during 1959 with a full front and forward entrance for one-man operation and became known locally as 'conkerboxes'. 557 remained in service until September 1969. *Omnicolour*

Soon to depart from Salisbury bus station for Shaftesbury on service 27 during October 1965 is Bristol LWL5G 554 (KWV 934). It was converted for one-man operation during November 1959 and remained in service for a further 10 years following its modifications.
*Colin Caddy*

together with semi-coach seating for the Salisbury-Southampton route. A start was made at the end of the year in equipping the 1952-54 Bristol LS6Gs for OMO, a programme which continued through 1958/59 and increased the supply of vehicles available for these duties.

After being part of the W&D scene for more than 27 years, the very last Leyland Titan, 145 (AHR 400), was withdrawn from passenger service on 24 March 1957, thus bringing to an end the company's long association with this once ubiquitous type.

A striking experimental coach livery was tried out on Bristol LS 543 in November 1957 when it was repainted cream with its roof, window surrounds and wings picked out in maroon. It remained in this guise until August 1958 but re-emerged in W&Ds newly adopted red and cream coach livery.

A start was made during 1958 to convert the 1954 Bristol LWLs to forward-entrance OMO vehicles. The first of these, 564, was converted at ECW during July 1958 but retained its half-cab and exposed radiator and was fitted with a diagonal window in the front bulkhead to allow space for the ticket machine. This arrangement was found to be unworkable in practice and W&D treated the remaining 14 buses in its own workshops between 1958 and 1960, starting with Nos 560/1 at the end of the year. They were fitted with full fronts incorporating a slightly raised vented panel over the original radiator. The front bulkhead was removed to enable a more practical siting for the ticket machine. No 564 was the last to be done in March 1960, thus bringing this prototype in line with the rest of its 'conkerbox' sisters, as the type soon became known.

Very healthy programmes of excursions were also offered from Salisbury, Andover and Basingstoke during the 1958 summer season to such destinations as Dartmoor, the Isle of Wight, the Wye Valley, Stratford-upon-Avon, Whipsnade Zoo and London Airport among many others.

By 1958 the service network was well established and had changed little in substance since the late 1940s. However, during this time some of the routes had been renumbered and some revised linkings and curtailments

Capturing a once familiar sight in Salisbury City centre is Bristol Lodekka LD6B 612 (LMW 915) on local service 55 out to West Harnham. This bus, in common with most subsequent vehicles, was absorbed into the Hants & Dorset fleet in October 1972, having been numbered into a common numbering system a year earlier. *R. H. G. Simpson*

dual-purpose saloons wore the maroon, cream and red livery of the front-engined coaches. However, with the advent and increase of OMO duties, the maroon and red livery was retained for those vehicles performing this work, while vehicles used on coach duties were painted red below the windows and cream above and were adorned with a smart silver ECW winged emblem. This situation remained until the introduction of all-cream livery for coaches in 1962, whereupon the maroon and red colours disappeared in favour of red bus livery, with red and cream now signifying dual-purpose vehicles.

More OMO buses entered service during 1956 in the shape of a further dozen Bristol LS5G saloons which arrived between February and December. These were joined by another 13 Bristol Lodekkas of which seven were fitted with platform doors for country routes including the Salisbury-Weymouth service. The following year saw just two new Lodekkas arrive which also had platform doors

Bristol LS6G 532 (JHR 495) was captured on film in the lush rural setting of Woodgreen while working service 40 to Salisbury in May 1970. New in January 1953, this bus had its rear exit removed in March 1955 and was fitted for one-man operation in November 1958. It was renumbered 755 in 1971 and taken out of service during November of that year.
*Chris Aston*

took place in line with changing demand and operating efficiencies. These included the Salisbury-Andover service 76 which had been extended to Basingstoke and service 80 which had been extended from Salisbury and Andover to Newbury. New Salisbury city services to Bemerton Heath were introduced as new housing was developed in this area.

Four new Gardner-engined Bristol Lodekkas with platform doors and semi-coach seats were delivered during 1958, one for the Southampton route and three for the Bournemouth service.

The first new coaches for eight years, in the shape of six Bristol MW6Gs with ECW 39-seat coachwork arrived during June and July painted in red and cream coach livery, as were two additional MW6G coaches which joined the fleet during April 1959. Two more semi-coach-seated Bristol Lodekka LD6Gs with platform doors concluded the new vehicle intake for the year and arrived in September and November.

A new joint service with the Bristol Omnibus Company started in June 1959 between Salisbury and Swindon. Numbered 709, it amalgamated Bristol's service 70 between Swindon and Marlborough with W&D's service 9 between Salisbury and Marlborough.

No new vehicles were purchased during 1960 but the following year six more Bristol MW6G coaches together with five MW6G OMO saloons with seating for 43 passengers arrived.

June 1962 saw the opening of a new bus station at Basingstoke with its platforms built to 'saw tooth' design. Provision was also made for layover spaces and for workshops in the complex. During the summer season a programme of excursions was run from Basingstoke as well as from Andover, Amesbury, Pewsey, Tidworth and Salisbury to a wide selection of places both in surrounding counties and further afield. Indeed, these excursions made use of the newly reliveried MW6G coaches which had hitherto operated in red and cream. They were now freshly painted in all-over cream with maroon wings; red and cream was now only applied to dual-purpose vehicles. These coaches were joined in May by three very modern

This line-up of Bristol MW6G coaches shows these vehicles in the cream livery with maroon wings which was adopted during 1962 in place of red and cream. Nearest the camera is 703 (RMR 524), delivered in July 1958. *R. H. G. Simpson*

Having just left Southampton bus station on its way back to Salisbury is 801 (XMR 948), the first MW6G service bus purchased by Wilts & Dorset. Delivered in August 1961, its ECW body seated 43. *R. H. G. Simpson*

Bristol MW6G 705 (RMR 992) started out as a 39-seat red and cream-liveried coach in July 1958. However, during 1967 it was rebuilt as shown with bus indicators, central exit and red livery and remained unique in the fleet, later being renumbered 805 and passing to Hants & Dorset. It was photographed in Salisbury bus station soon after conversion as it awaited its next duty. *John Hypher*

702 (RHR 853) is a dual-purpose Bristol MW6G seen at Southampton coach station during the summer of 1968 having dropped off a private hire party. Its former cream livery gave way to red and cream during 1967 and at the same time it received bus-style indicators. New in June 1958, it was later renumbered 802 before being transferred to Hants & Dorset. *John Hypher*

Another variation of predominantly red livery is pictured on 807 (SWV 688), former MW6G coach 707 dating from April 1959. It was modified to dual-purpose status, as shown, in 1968 before receiving its red roof. *Photobus*

Bristol MW6G coaches of a totally new design by ECW. With seating for 39 passengers, they had curved glass windscreens and curved rear windows as well as glass cant panels. They were painted cream with red waistbands with their fleetnames placed at the leading end of the bands in cream plastic lettering and were the first W&D vehicles to carry reversed registration numbers.

Express coach services had continued to be developed during the early and mid 1950s, and by 1962 were departing from 24 military camps to numerous destinations in England, together with services to Edinburgh and Glasgow as well as to Bristol for rail

connections to South Wales. The value and success of these services was very important to W&D and each week bookings were taken at each camp by visiting company representatives.

Other new vehicles arriving during the year were a further five Bristol MW6G saloons together with the first Bristol FS-type Lodekkas which featured completely flat lower deck floors, a new design of radiator grille, platform doors and semi-coach seats. Of the 13 new Lodekkas, ten were FS6Gs with Gardner engines while the remainder had Bristol BVW engines and were designated FS6B. The arrival of these buses enabled a cascading of vehicles

Open platform Bristol
Lodekka FS6B 653
(691 AAM) leaves
Basingstoke bus station
on local town service 128
to Brackley Way.
New in April 1963,
the characteristic black
lining-out to its cream
bands gives the livery a
smart and crisp appearance.
*R. H. G. Simpson*

At a foot longer than the
original batch of these
attractively designed
ECW-bodied Bristol MW6G
coaches, 719 (131 AMW)
was one of three to join the
fleet in November 1962.
Its simple livery of cream
with red relief suits these
coaches well.
*R. H. G. Simpson*

to take place which saw the last of the ex-Venture AEC Regents taken out of service at Basingstoke in September. Three further Bristol MW6G coaches of the new design joined the fleet in November but at 31ft were a foot longer than their sisters, giving their 39 passengers a little more leg room.

The 1962 Transport Act brought the dissolution of the British Transport Commission and vested the Government's road passenger transport interests in its successor, the Transport Holding Company (THC). This change of ownership brought no outward changes to the fleet or publicity.

At the end of 1962, Mr Raymond Longman retired from Wilts & Dorset after a long career with the company spanning some 42 years, most of which were at the most senior level. He guided the company through peacetime and war and maintained a profitability which many other companies envied. He was always conscious too that it was the staff of all grades that helped make W&D the success it was and for many years led the board in proposing a Christmas bonus for all employees from apprentices to managers. His place was taken by a new director and general manager, David Deacon, who had come from United Automobile Services at Darlington where he held

The Salisbury-Bournemouth route, run jointly with Hants & Dorset, was one of W&D's longest established services. It carried various route numbers over the years but it was the 38 which became synonymous with this service to the end. Bristol LD6G Lodekka 633 (RWV 526) was a regular performer on this route and is seen picking up passengers at Christchurch Town Hall *en route* to Salisbury in August 1961. It passed to Hants & Dorset, having previously been renumbered 433. *Omnicolour*

With their new fleetnumbers 10 and 8 respectively, 132 and 130 AMW are Bristol MW6G coaches with new-style ECW bodies with seating for 39. Formerly numbered 720 and 718, they were new in November 1962 and were photographed at Salisbury depot during October 1971. Alongside is a Ribble Leyland Leopard/Plaxton Elite on a Southern Tour. *David Mant*

Looking splendid in its simple, yet effective coach colours, Bristol MW6G 720 (132 AMW) is seen at Porthmadog on tour in July 1971. *Colin Caddy*

the post of traffic manager and assistant general manager.

1963 was the year that the well-known Wiltshire independent Silver Star disappeared from the scene after 40 years of service. 'The Star' had sold out to Wilts & Dorset and ran its last service from Salisbury to Porton on the evening of 4 June, with W&D taking over the following day. Silver Star had been formed in September 1923 by Eddie Shergold and Ben White, who started a service from Salisbury via the Winterbournes and Porton to Allington with vehicles based at their depot at Porton. They introduced another service from Salisbury to Sling three years later, but sold this to Wilts & Dorset in 1937. In addition to its stage services, the Star also ran coach excursions from the camps at Porton and Bulford.

During 1949 the company took over the Salisbury-East Gomeldon service from Lee of Winterbourne Gunner and in 1952 started to run weekend leave express services to London from Bulford and Porton camps and from Winterbourne. Over the next three years, Silver Star coaches were to be seen far and wide as they ran additional express services from Bulford Camp to South Wales, the Midlands, the North West, the North East and Scotland. In contrast, a new local express service began in 1957 from Bemerton Heath for workers at Porton Camp.

During the same year, the Star adopted one-man operation with Harrington-bodied Leyland Tiger Cubs, as it felt the effects of declining passenger numbers. Until 1957 the legal title of the company had been Shergold & White

Ltd, trading as Silver Star, but this was changed to Silver Star Motor Services Ltd. Soon after the death of Eddie Shergold in October 1962, the decision was taken to sell the Star and it passed to W&D the following June.

For many years, the Silver Star fleet consisted mainly of Leyland vehicles, including four of the modern rear-engined Atlantean double-deckers. The sale included the Allington stage service, the Bemerton Heath-Porton express service and 16 forces' weekend leave express services together with the fleet of 23 buses and coaches. W&D retained just nine Leyland saloons and coaches,

six Tiger Cubs, one Royal Tiger and two Leopards, all with Harrington bodies. The balance were sold to Western National, Bristol Omnibus Company and Super of Upminster. It is a pity that the Atlanteans were not taken into W&D stock as they would have looked splendid in W&D livery and would have raised the profile of the double-deck fleet. Instead, three passed to Bristol and one went to Super at Upminster.

New purchases during the year included a further seven Bristol FS6B Lodekkas with open platforms and a pair of 41-seat dual-purpose Bristol MW6G saloons painted red

Pictured in Salisbury City centre on its usual route to Winterbourne and Allington is Silver Star Leyland Tiger Cub 31 (PHR 829) with 41-seat Harrington coachwork. When Silver Star was acquired by Wilts & Dorset in June 1963, this vehicle was numbered 901.
*R. H. G. Simpson*

A picture of what might have been if W&D had retained the four Silver Star rear-engined Leyland Atlanteans. Coach-seated 40 (XMW 706) was acquired with the Silver Star business in June 1963, but was sold to Super of Upminster without turning a wheel for Wilts & Dorset.
*R. H. G. Simpson*

Former Silver Star Leyland Leopard L1 with Harrington coachwork 908 (WAM 441) is seen passing the rear of Salisbury bus station as it sets out for Weymouth on service 34 during August 1970. This vehicle was just three years old when acquired with the Silver Star business in 1963 and remained in service until May 1972, by which time it had been renumbered 998. *David Gillard*

Leyland Tiger Cub PSUC1/2 903 (RAM 620), bodied by Harrington, started life with Silver Star in 1958. It was one of nine Harrington-bodied Leylands retained by Wilts & Dorset from that fleet, bringing a return of this once numerous marque to the company. Bournemouth bus station acts as host to 903 during August 1963. Bearing its new fleetnumber 996, it was withdrawn in February 1972. *Omnicolour*

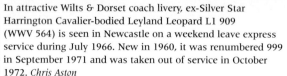

In attractive Wilts & Dorset coach livery, ex-Silver Star Harrington Cavalier-bodied Leyland Leopard L1 909 (WWV 564) is seen in Newcastle on a weekend leave express service during July 1966. New in 1960, it was renumbered 999 in September 1971 and was taken out of service in October 1972. *Chris Aston*

▲

A later view of Leyland Leopard 909 (WWV 564), but now numbered 999 shows it in dual-purpose livery with pay-as-you-enter sign which it received in February 1970. Photographed in July 1972 at Winchester, this former member of the Silver Star fleet was just three months away from withdrawal. *David Mant*

▶▶

and cream. October saw the arrival of another new type of double-decker into the fleet, the first pair of forward-entrance, 70-seat Bristol FLF6G Lodekkas which featured electrically-operated four-piece jack-knife doors controlled by the driver. These were the longest double-deckers in the fleet, at 30ft.

David Deacon's tenure as director and general manager was a short one, as during early 1964 he was appointed to the Tilling Group board. The opportunity was taken to place both Wilts & Dorset and Hants & Dorset under common management and Douglas Morison, the director and general manager of Hants & Dorset, assumed overall control of both companies from April. This move was the beginning of the end for W&D and although no immediate changes took place, the writing was on the wall.

A further four forward-entrance Bristol FLF6G Lodekkas were delivered during the year of which two, delivered in August and September, were the first examples in the fleet to carry the new letter 'B' year suffixes to their registration numbers. These were joined by another eight Bristol FS6B Lodekkas with platform doors, the last member of which also carried a 'B'-suffix registration.

New coaches for 1965 were a complete departure from the more usual Bristol/ECW vehicles, with five lightweight Bedford SB13s with Duple 41-seat bodies joining the fleet between April and July. These also carried plastic fleetnames together with a broad red band and red window surrounds.

At the end of 1965, the registered offices of both Wilts & Dorset and Venture were moved to Hants & Dorset's address of The Square, Bournemouth, thus drawing to a close the company's official connection with Salisbury. Legal lettering on W&D's vehicles displayed the new address from this time.

Bedford SB13 914 (BMW 139C) with Duple 41-seat coachwork was photographed at Crosville's Liverpool depot during November 1969, having worked to the city on a servicemen's weekend leave express service from Salisbury Plain. New in July 1965, this coach did not remain in the fleet for long; it was withdrawn in January 1972. *Mark Hughes*

Pictured at Basingstoke is Bristol FLF6G Lodekka 674 (EMR 290D) with ECW 70-seat bodywork. Although the central cream band is still lined-out in black, the upper cream band has been discontinued. Cave-Brown-Cave heating is installed, which eliminates the need for the traditional radiator. Engine cooling and saloon heating are achieved by means of the intakes each side of the destination display. *Maurice Doggett*

Bedford buses started to be purchased alongside the more traditional Bristols from 1967. All but one were bodied by Willowbrook, but this solitary example, 813 (HHR 943E), dating from March 1967 was bodied by Strachans with seating for 33 passengers and standing room for a further 25. *Maurice Doggett*

One of the FS6G Lodekkas, No 646, was repainted all-over cream with maroon wings in early 1966 for new limited-stop service 38A between Salisbury and Bournemouth which ran jointly with Hants & Dorset via Ferndown instead of Christchurch. Although dedicated to this service and painted as a coach, it was not upgraded with coach seats but retained the semi-coach seating with which it was delivered.

The new vehicle intake during the year comprised ten more forward-entrance Bristol FLF Lodekkas, five dual-purpose Bristol MW6G saloons and a pair of MW6G standard saloons. These were followed in 1967 by five more Bedford coaches, together with a pair of Bedford saloons and a further 10 Bristol FLFs, the very last double-deckers to enter service with Wilts & Dorset. The Bedford VAM14 coaches were bodied by Duple Northern and carried 41 seats whereas the two VAM14 buses were bodied by two different coachbuilders, Strachans and Willowbrook. These two buses featured dual doors with seating for 33 passengers and standing room for a further 25. Of the Lodekkas, five were powered by Bristol engines while the remainder were supplied unusually with Leyland O.600 units, and were designated FLF6L. All ten had semi-automatic gearboxes, the first such units in the fleet, which produced a range of distinctive high-pitched sounds.

A new type of coach entered service with W&D during 1968. These were high capacity Bedford VAL70s, which featured twin steering axles, with Duple Northern 49-seat bodies, four of which joined the company in April. At 36ft, these were the longest vehicles in the fleet and heralded the start of maximum-size buses and coaches. Another six twin-door Bedford VAM saloons with Willowbrook 40-seat bodies arrived in June concluding the intake for the year.

The National Bus Company (NBC) was brought into being on 1 January 1969 under the 1968 Transport Act and brought together the Tilling Group of companies owned by THC and the UK bus interests of BET which had been acquired by the state. BTC and later the THC also held substantial interests in the BET companies via the railway companies and all of these were vested in the new National Bus Company.

One of the very last new double-deckers to be purchased by Wilts & Dorset was 688 (JMR 818F), a Bristol FLF6L Lodekka with semi-automatic transmission which entered service in October 1967. It was photographed at Salisbury bus station before setting out for Trowbridge on service 24.
*Author's Collection*

The first three-axle Bedford VAL70s joined the coach fleet during 1968. This example, 922 (LMR 733F), with Duple Northern 49-seat coachwork was delivered during April and continues a trend of carrying a greater area of red within its cream paintwork.
*Maurice Doggett*

Pictured at Cheltenham coach station in September 1972 is 16 (HAM 501E), a Bedford VAM14 with Duple Northern 41-seat coachwork. This coach entered service in March 1967 as number 915 and passed to Hants & Dorset a month after this photo was taken. *Mark Hughes*

▲

Since 1965 Bedford buses and coaches featured quite significantly in Wilts & Dorset's new vehicle intake. This Bedford VAM70 (LMR 739F) with dual-door Willowbrook body entered service in June 1968 as No 819 and received its present number, 507, in September 1971. It is seen *en route* to Amesbury with military vehicles behind, a common sight around Salisbury Plain. *Photobus*

Bristol MW6G 725 (EMR 300D) climbs Dorchester High Street *en route* to Weymouth during July 1970 on service 34 from Salisbury. *Omnicolour*

Formerly numbered 811, EMR 303D has carried its new fleetnumber since September 1971. A Bristol MW6G with ECW coachwork, this bus entered service during September 1966 and stands at Salisbury bus station awaiting departure for Devizes in 1971. *Photobus*

Fresh out of paintshops is 207 (EMR 288D) a Bristol FLF6G forward-entrance Lodekka with seating for 70 passengers. Since its arrival as number 672 in January 1966, this bus has received a replacement Hants & Dorset radiator grille and as this October 1972 photograph shows, has had its mudguards painted red. In view of its transfer to Hants & Dorset at this time, it was thankfully outshopped with traditional Wilts & Dorset fleetnames, though the National Bus Company advert on the side has portents of things to come. *David Mant*

Three-axle Bedford VAL70 14 (LMR 734F) with a Duple Northern 49-seat body is seen carrying a party to Butlins at Filey. This coach entered service in April 1968 with fleet number 923 in the then W&D coach series. *Photobus*

Wilts & Dorset enjoyed just five months as a 'proper' subsidiary of NBC before being legally absorbed into Hants & Dorset from 1 June. It now became merely a trading name of H&D and this was reflected in the revised legal lettering which became Hants & Dorset Motor Services Ltd, trading as Wilts & Dorset Motor Services, The Square, Bournemouth.

Twenty-four new vehicles were delivered through 1969 which included two new types of single-deck buses from Bristol and ECW. Interestingly, the new H&D ownership was reflected in most of the registration numbers, which from now on bore Bournemouth marks rather than the usual Wiltshire letters. The first rear-engined buses to enter service comprised 14 36ft semi-automatic Bristol RELL6Gs with dual doors and seating for 45 passengers and standing room for a further 23. By contrast, the other new type comprised six shorter-length, lightweight, dual-door, underfloor-engined Bristol LH6Ls which seated 39 with provision for 12 standees. Another four Bedford VAL70 coaches with 49-seat Duple Northern bodies bolstered the

The first batch of rear-engined Bristol RELL6G saloons with ECW dual-door bodies arrived during the spring of 1969. 824 (MMW 354G) entered service in May and was photographed while still new running to Salisbury. This bus was renumbered 604 a couple of years later in 1971. *Chris Aston*

Formerly a Bristol Lodekka stronghold, service 38 is seen here at Christchurch being worked by rear-engined Bristol RELL6G 608 (PRU 63G) with dual-door ECW bodywork. Formerly numbered 828, this bus entered service in June 1969 and is heading towards Bournemouth.
*R. H. G. Simpson*

Pictured at Newbury is dual-door ECW-bodied Bristol LH6L 840 (RRU 694H) awaiting its return to Salisbury. This vehicle entered service in January 1970.
*Maurice Doggett*

Dual-purpose 50-seat Bristol RELL6G 605 (MMW 355G) rests at Salisbury bus station with a former Silver Star Leyland Tiger Cub approaching from behind. It was new in May 1969 as 825. *Photobus*

Dual-door Bristol LH6L 523 (REL 748H), with ECW 39-seat body, drops off passengers at Salisbury bus station having travelled in from Weymouth during September 1972. This bus entered service three years earlier in September 1969 carrying fleet number 837. As a result of the company being administered by Hants & Dorset, Bournemouth registrations have now started to be allocated rather than Wiltshire marks. *Mark Hughes*

coach fleet and were of a squarer, sleeker design featuring substantial areas of red plus a wide fluted chrome band below the windows finished off with cream roofs and skirting. These vehicles, in common with all recent coaches, carried plastic fleetnames positioned towards the leading ends of the vehicles. More of the same arrived in 1970, a further three Bedford VAL70/Duple coaches, four more Bristol RELL6G 'standee' saloons and an additional four 'standee' Bristol LH6Ls. These were supplemented by the surprising transfer of four elderly front-engined Bristol

LL6B OMO saloons with full-fronted 37-seat ECW bodies from H&D.

A further step towards full integration with Hants & Dorset was a fleetwide renumbering which took place in September 1971. Up to now, both fleets continued to be numbered separately using their own systems but a new scheme was devised whereby W&D-allocated vehicles received three-figure numbers depending on type, while H&D vehicles were given similar numbers plus 1000. For example, the first W&D-liveried FLF Lodekka was

This dual-purpose, rear-engined, Bristol RELL6G with ECW bodywork 846 (TRU 947J) has seating for 50 passengers and entered service in January 1971. They were regular performers on the Swindon service. *Maurice Doggett Collection*

850 (UEL 567J) is a single-door ECW-bodied Bristol LH6L photographed at Salisbury when new at the end of October 1970 before entering service in November. *David Mant*

Dual-purpose Bristol RELL6G 621 (TRU 948J) passes through Swindon and overtakes a Thamesdown Transport Daimler Fleetline on its way out to Savernake Hospital in September 1972. Notice the curved windscreen on this vehicle compared with the flat screens of similar vehicles illustrated elsewhere. *Mark Hughes*

numbered 201, while the first similar H&D Lodekka received the number 1201.

Just seven new vehicles were allocated to W&D during 1971, the first of which were three single-entrance Bristol RELL6Gs with ECW dual-purpose 50-seat bodies painted red and cream. These were followed by four coaches comprising a pair of Bedford YRQs with 41-seat coachwork by Duple and another pair of elegant Duple-bodied Bedford VAL70s seating 49.

More secondhand Leylands joined those already in

service from Silver Star in the shape of two rear-engined Leyland Panthers which came from Maidstone & District. They carried 49-seat BET-style Willowbrook bodies and were still relatively new, dating from 1967. Another 14 provided half of the final vehicle intake during 1972, some still in the dark green of their former owner with W&D fleetnames. One Bristol LS5G saloon and two Bristol MW6G coaches were also transferred across the fleets from H&D. The very last new buses to be delivered in full W&D livery consisted of six Bristol LH6L single-door, 43-seat

The penultimate Bedford VAL70 to be delivered to Wilts & Dorset was 62 (WEL 802J) with this sleek 49-seat Duple Viceroy 37 body. It was photographed at Salisbury just three days after entering service in July 1971. *David Mant*

Still carrying Maidstone & District green livery is 685 (JKK 196E), a Leyland Panther with Willowbrook 49-seat bodywork. Acquired during 1972 and entering service in September, it is setting out from Bournemouth bus station for Salisbury. It is seen alongside sister vehicle 1691 in the Hants & Dorset fleet. Although it has a traditional Wilts & Dorset fleetname on the front, it also has red NBC-style fleetnames on the cove panels. *Chris Aston*

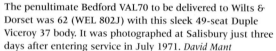

Former Maidstone & District Leyland Panther with Willowbrook body 686 (JKK 197E) had been repainted into Wilts & Dorset livery when photographed at Basingstoke bus station in May 1972 just a couple of months after entering service. *David Mant*

Looking splendid in red is this former Hants & Dorset Bristol LL6B with cutaway rear for the Sandbanks Ferry which was transferred in August 1970 and was photographed at Salisbury before entering service. Its chassis was new in 1950 and received this ECW body during 1962. 595 (KEL 408) only remained with W&D for a couple of years, being renumbered 723 in 1971 and taken out of service in July 1972.
*David Mant*

PRIVATE PROPERTY
NO ENTRY
EXCEPT FOR BUS
PASSENGERS

WILTS & DORSET

FEL 424D

EMPLOYMENT EXCH

saloons together with another three dual-purpose Bristol RELL6Gs, and finally, an additional pair of dual-door Bristol RELL6G 'standee' saloons.

February 1972 saw the closure of Amesbury depot, with its operations being transferred to Pewsey and Salisbury. It is surprising that a small outstation was not retained, as operating efficiencies must have been compromised significantly by wasteful dead mileage and crew time. Blandford depot was also downgraded to outstation status in February, with part of the building later used as a paintshop.

Full integration with Hants & Dorset took place on 1 October 1972 when a start was made replacing all W&D fleetnames with those of Hants & Dorset in NBC style with 'double N' logos. However Wilts & Dorset was to retain one lasting legacy. NBC offered a choice of leaf green or poppy red and white livery with grey wheels; green would have seemed the logical choice for Hants & Dorset, but instead red was adopted for the entire combined bus fleet, with coaches gaining National white livery with large red and blue fleetnames and 'double N' logos.

And so, after 58 years, Wilts & Dorset faded from the scene, although to many its history, its buildings, its staff, its routes and its vehicles will continue to live on in their memories.

▲ The sole example of the later ECW MW coach body with a deeper flush windscreen in the W&D fleet was 12 (FEL 424D), a Bristol MW6G transferred from Hants & Dorset in January 1972. It was photographed at Salisbury bus station in September of that year. *Mark Hughes*

◀◀ Another vehicle transferred from Hants & Dorset and pictured at Salisbury bus station in September 1972 was Bristol LS5G 1783 (SRU 973) painted into W&D livery. Just a month later Wilts & Dorset ceased to exist, although the name remained a while longer until fleetnames were replaced by those of Hants & Dorset. *David Mant*

◀ The fleet renumbering into a common series with Hants & Dorset took place in September 1971. Bristol FLF6G 662 (AHR 244B) is seen having its old fleetnumber plate painted over at Salisbury on 4 September and replaced by its new number 205 (almost!) depicted in yellow. *Both: David Mant*

# 5. POSTSCRIPT

The Wilts & Dorset name was not however destined to disappear into oblivion. It was resurrected after an absence of 11 years when Hants & Dorset was split into a number of self-standing smaller units. The new Wilts & Dorset was created on 1 April 1983 and embraced all Poole-area routes together with services based on Swanage, Ringwood, Lymington, Blandford, Pewsey and Salisbury. Services in the Andover and Basingstoke areas became part of the newly created Hampshire Bus.

It will be seen that only a part of the former Wilts & Dorset territory was included in the new company, a significant proportion of its area having its roots in the 'old' Hants & Dorset company. In the privatisation of NBC, Wilts & Dorset was sold to its management team on 24 June 1987. In August 2004, the company was sold again, this time to the Go-Ahead Group who have retained the company name and which is currently developing new services, liveries and brandings and introducing new high-capacity vehicles across their area.

And Hants & Dorset also survives: as a subsidiary of Wilts & Dorset, trading as Damory Coaches!

Wilts & Dorset as it is today. The location is Poole, now Wilts & Dorset's heartland but formerly in Hants & Dorset-land. One of the first double-deckers painted in the latest livery was this Optare Spectra, 3101, with a Volvo B7RLE in the 'more' livery adopted initially for Poole-Bournemouth services. Wilts & Dorset is still active in and around Salisbury, which is almost an entirely separate operation.
*Stephen Morris*

# APPENDIX 1 SERVICES OPERATING OCTOBER 1935

1     Salisbury-Amesbury
2     Salisbury-Larkhill-Shrewton
3     Salisbury-Larkhill via Bulford Camp and Durrington
4     Salisbury-Devizes
5     Salisbury-Marlborough
6     Salisbury-Netheravon RAF Station
7     Salisbury-Tidworth via Cholderton
8     Salisbury-Amesbury-Andover
9     Andover-Marlborough
10    Andover-Appleshaw-Redenham
11    Andover-Broughton-Houghton Corner
12    Andover-Newbury
13    Andover-Hungerford
14    Salisbury-Romsey via Whiteparish
      (change at Whiteparish)
15    Salisbury-Romsey via Lockerley
16    Salisbury-Southampton (joint with Hants & Dorset)
17    Salisbury-Bournemouth (joint with Hants & Dorset)
17A   Salisbury-Rockbourne-Fordingbridge
17B   Fordingbridge-Woodgreen-Breamore
17C   Fordingbridge-Hyde
18    Salisbury-Downton-Woodfalls
18A   Woodfalls Cross-Redlynch-Morgans Vale Corner
19    Andover-Romsey
20    Salisbury-Weymouth (joint with Southern National)
21    Salisbury-Shaftesbury
22    Salisbury-Coombe Bissett
23    Salisbury-Netherhampton
24    Salisbury-Trowbridge
25    Salisbury-Shaftesbury via Fovant
26    Andover-Salisbury via The Wallops
27    Salisbury-Woodfords-Amesbury
27A   Salisbury-Great Durnford
28    Salisbury-Old Sarum Aerodrome
29    Woodfalls-Plaitford
30    Tidworth-Andover
31    Upavon Village-Upavon RAF Camp

**Salisbury City Services (un-numbered)**
Market-St Marks Church
Market-Laverstock
Market-West Harnham
Market-Meyrick Avenue
Market-Waters Road
Market-Devizes Road
Market-Wilton-Ditchampton

**Andover Town Services (un-numbered)**
Guildhall-Amport
Guildhall-Wilton Road
Guildhall-Charlton-Hatherden-Tangley
Guildhall-Lower Clatford

▲ Photographed before entering service is 112 (WV 2382), a Leyland Titan TD2 with a Leyland 48-seat body. It entered service in January 1933 and received a Leyland oil engine five years later before being rebodied by Wilts & Dorset in March 1944. This bus remained in service for a commendable 22 years before being withdrawn in January 1955.
*Phil Davies Collection*

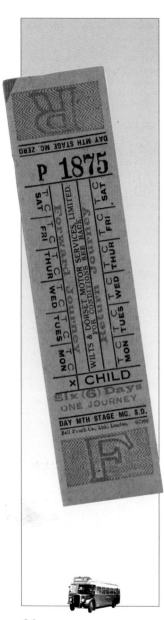

| | | | |
|---|---|---|---|
| 1 | Salisbury-Amesbury via Woodford | 41 | Fordingbridge-Hyde |
| 2 | Salisbury-Larkhill-Shrewton | 42 | Salisbury-Cranbourne |
| 3 | Salisbury-Bulford-Larkhill | 43 | Salisbury-Fordingbridge direct |
| 4 | Salisbury-Old Sarum | 44 | Salisbury-Woodfalls |
| 5 | Salisbury-Marlborough | 45 | Woodfalls-Nomansland |
| 6 | Salisbury-Netheravon | 46 | Salisbury-Netherhampton |
| 7 | Salisbury-Boscombe Down | 54 | Salisbury Market-Laverstock |
| 8 | Salisbury-Tidworth-Andover | 55 | Salisbury Market-West Harnham |
| 9 | Salisbury-Winterbourne-Tidworth | 56 | Salisbury Market-Milton Road |
| 10 | Salisbury-Devizes | 57 | Salisbury Market-Meyrick Avenue |
| 11 | Devizes-Easterton | 58 | Salisbury Market-Coronation Avenue |
| 12 | Devizes-Beechingstoke | 59 | Salisbury Market-Heath Road |
| 13 | Devizes-Ablington-Salisbury | 60 | Salisbury Market-Wilton |
| 14 | Devizes-Andover | 61 | Salisbury Market-Waters Road |
| 15 | Devizes-Burbage | 62 | Salisbury Market-St Mark's |
| 16 | Pewsey-Hungerford | 70 | Andover-Rookesbury Road |
| 17 | Pewsey-Marlborough | 71 | Andover-Amport |
| 18 | Pewsey-Upavon | 72 | Andover-Marlborough |
| 19 | Salisbury-Blandford via Camp | 73 | Andover-Redenham |
| 20 | Salisbury-Weymouth (joint with Southern National) | 74 | Andover-Perham Down |
| 21 | Blandford-Blandford Camp | 75 | Andover-Kimpton-Tidworth |
| 22 | Blandford-Tarrant Rushton | 76 | Andover-Wallop-Salisbury |
| 24 | Salisbury-Trowbridge | 77 | Andover-Broughton |
| 25 | Salisbury-Mere | 78 | Andover-Abbotts Ann |
| 26 | Salisbury-Hindon | 79 | Andover-Lower Clatford |
| 27 | Salisbury-Shaftesbury direct | 80 | Andover-Newbury |
| 28 | Salisbury-Tisbury-Shaftesbury | 81 | Andover-Hungerford |
| 29 | Salisbury-Bowerchalke-Shaftesbury | 82 | Andover-Tangley |
| 30 | Salisbury-Coombe Bissett | 83 | Andover-Romsey |
| 32 | Salisbury-Winterslow direct | | |
| 33 | Salisbury-Farley-Winterslow | | |
| 35 | Salisbury-Whiteparish-Romsey | | |
| 36 | Salisbury-Lockerley-Romsey | | |
| 37 | Salisbury-Southampton (joint with Hants & Dorset) | | |
| 38 | Salisbury-Bournemouth (joint with Hants & Dorset) | | |
| 39 | Fordingbridge-Rockbourne | | |
| 40 | Fordingbridge-Woodgreen-Salisbury | | |

# APPENDIX 3  SERVICES OPERATING MAY 1962

1 Salisbury-Woodfords-Durnford-Amesbury
2 Salisbury-Larkhill-Shrewton-Tilshead
3 Salisbury-Bulford-Larkhill
4 Salisbury-Old Sarum RAF
5 Salisbury-Upavon-Marlborough
6 Salisbury-Durrington-Netheravon
7 Salisbury-Boscombe Down
8 Salisbury-Amesbury-Tidworth-Andover
9 Salisbury-Tidworth-Marlborough-Chiseldon-Swindon (also 709)
10 Salisbury-Upavon-Devizes
11 Devizes-Urchfont
12 Pewsey-Beechingstoke-Devizes
13 Salisbury-Ablington-Netheravon RAF
14 Marlborough-Bedwyn-Oxenwood-Andover
15 Hungerford-Oxenwood-Vernham Dean-Andover
16 Pewsey-Hungerford
17 Marlborough-Wexcombe-Oxenwood-Andover
18 Upavon-Upavon RAF-Tidworth
19 Marlborough-Burbage-Ludgershall-Andover
20 Devizes-Bishops Cannings
21 Blandford-Blandford Camp
23 Warminster-Sutton Veny
24 Salisbury-Warminster-Trowbridge
25 Salisbury-Hindon-Mere-Zeals
26 Salisbury-Tisbury-Hindon
27 Salisbury-Shaftesbury direct
28 Salisbury-Tisbury-Shaftesbury
29 Salisbury-Bowerchalke-Shaftesbury
30 Salisbury-Coombe Bissett
31 Tisbury-Newtown
32 Salisbury-Winterslow direct
33 Salisbury-Farley-Winterslow
34 Salisbury-Pimperne-Blandford-Weymouth (joint with Southern National)
35 Blandford-Collingwood Corner via Camp
36 Salisbury-Lockerley-Romsey

37 Salisbury-Southampton (joint with Hants & Dorset)
38 Salisbury-Bournemouth (joint with Hants & Dorset)
39 Salisbury-Rockbourne-Fordingbridge
40 Salisbury-Woodgreen-Fordingbridge
41 Fordingbridge-Hyde
42 Salisbury-Cranborne
44 Salisbury-Woodfalls-Redlynch-Hale
45 Salisbury-Woodfalls-Nomansland
51 Salisbury City Centre-Woodside Road-Bemerton Heath
52 Salisbury City Centre-The Valley-Bemerton Heath
53 Salisbury City Centre-Skew Bridge-Bemerton Heath
54 Salisbury City Centre-Laverstock via St Marks Church
55 Salisbury City Centre-West Harnham
56 Salisbury City Centre-Netherhampton
57 Salisbury City Centre-Meyrick Avenue
59 Salisbury City Centre-Devizes Road Prefabs
60 Salisbury City Centre-Wilton-Ditchampton-Bulbridge

▲ Leyland Lion LT1 77 (MW 6285) was delivered in January 1930 with a Leyland 35-seat body. However, the body shown here was supplied by Beadle during May 1947 and built on to the reconditioned chassis which had been fitted with the longer 'Cov-Rad' radiator illustrated. Pictured at Salisbury bus station and soon to depart for Shaftesbury, this bus remained in service until February 1953. *Maurice Doggett Collection/Surfleet*

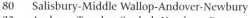

The mixture of AEC double-deckers, saloons and coaches taken over from Venture in January 1951 included this especially handsome 1948 AEC Regal III coach with Duple 35-seat bodywork. 492 (GCG 544) remained in the coach fleet until September 1958.
*Maurice Doggett Collection*

▲ 61 Salisbury City Centre-Waters Road
62 Salisbury City Centre-St Marks Avenue-Bishopdown Estate
63 Salisbury City Centre-London Road-Bishopdown Estate
64 Salisbury City Centre-Butt's Farm Estate-St Francis Road
65 Salisbury City Centre-Laverstock via Milford Hill
66 Salisbury-Romsey-Winchester (joint with Hants & Dorset)
67 Salisbury City Centre-Quidhampton-Ditchampton
68 Andover-Winchester (joint with Hants & Dorset)
69 Andover Town Guildhall-Tollgate Road-King George Road
70 Andover Town Hedge End Road-Guildhall-Rooksbury Road-King George Rd
71 Andover-Amport
72 Andover Town Bus Station-Picket Piece
73 Andover-Redenham-Upper Chute/Tidworth
75 Andover-Kimpton-Tidworth
76 Salisbury-Middle Wallop-Andover-Basingstoke
77 Andover-Abbotts Ann-Broughton
79 Andover-Lower Clatford

80 Salisbury-Middle Wallop-Andover-Newbury
82 Andover-Tangley-Conholt-Vernham Dean
83 Andover-Stockbridge-Romsey
101 Basingstoke-Sherfield-Bramley Camp-Bramley Village
102 Basingstoke-Longparish-Andover
103 Basingstoke-Worting-Oakley
104 Whitchurch-Overton Mills
105 Baughurst-Pamber-Bramley Camp
106 Basingstoke Town Grove Road-Bus Station-Hatch Lane
107 Basingstoke-Herriard-Wield-Alton
108 Basingstoke Town Queen Mary Avenue-Bus Station-Golden Lion
109 Basingstoke-Ellisfield-Alresford-Cheriton
111 Basingstoke-North Waltham-Winchester
112 Basingstoke Town South Ham-Kempshott
113 Basingstoke Town Thornycroft Works-Queen Mary Avenue
114 Basingstoke Town Thornycroft Works-Grove Road
115 Baughurst-Silchester-Bramley Camp
117 Basingstoke-Lyde Green
121 Basingstoke-Wootton-Hannington-Wolverton
122 Basingstoke-Kingsclere-Newbury (joint with Thames Valley)
125 Basingstoke Town Queen Mary Avenue-Bus Station-Western Way
126 Basingstoke Town Western Way-Bus Station-Queen Mary Avenue
127 Basingstoke Town Kempshott/Brackley Way-Bus Station-Park Prewett
128 Basingstoke Town Kempshott/Brackley Way-Bus Station-Oakridge Road
129 Basingstoke Town Bus Station-Worting-Roman Road/Kempshott
130 Basingstoke Town Bus Station-Roman Road/Kingsclere Road
134 Basingstoke-Silchester-Baughurst
135 Whitchurch-Burghclere Common-Newbury
136 Basingstoke-West Heath-Beenham
137 Basingstoke-Tadley-Baughurst

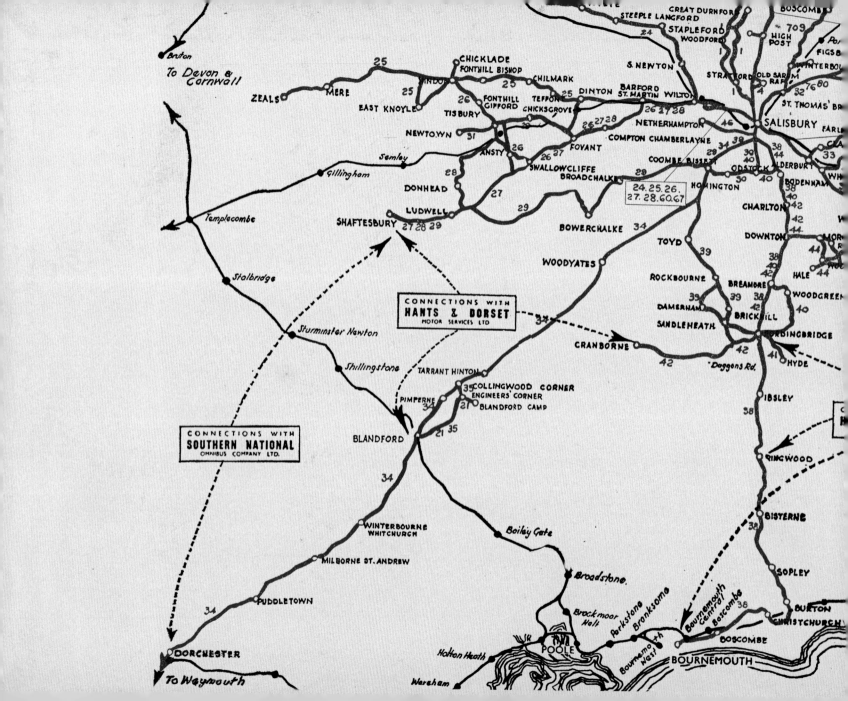